D1423449

THE CLAN MACKINTOSH
AND
THE CLAN CHATTAN

Official Emblazonment of Arms of the 29th Chief of Mackintosh.

THE CLAN MACKINTOSH
AND
THE CLAN CHATTAN

BY

MARGARET MACKINTOSH OF MACKINTOSH

FOREWORD BY

COLONEL SIR DONALD CAMERON OF LOCHIEL
K.T., C.M.G., A.D.C.

1948

W. & A. K. JOHNSTON LIMITED
EDINBURGH AND LONDON

Printed in Great Britain by W. & A. K. Johnston, Limited, Edinburgh

DEDICATED TO

MY HUSBAND

Rear Admiral

LACHLAN DONALD MACKINTOSH
OF MACKINTOSH

C.B., D.S.O., D.S.C.

without whose help and inspiration
this book could not have been written.

PREFACE

THE object of this book is to give a short history of the Mackintoshes and Clan Chattan, mainly from the Mackintosh aspect. A fully detailed history was written some years ago by Alistair Mackintosh, a cousin of the late Chief, from which I have obtained most of the information in this book. I also owe much to the manuscript of Alistair's wife, Florence, which was never published. Alistair's history was privately printed and only a few copies were circulated. I have also referred to Charles Fraser-Mackintosh's *Minor Septs of Clan Chattan*, and *Scottish Clans and Their Tartans*, published by Messrs W. & A. K. Johnston.

MARGARET MACKINTOSH OF MACKINTOSH.

MOY HALL,
INVERNESS-SHIRE.
1947.

CONTENTS

APPENDICES

MAPS

ILLUSTRATIONS

ILLUSTRATIONS IN COLOUR

TARTANS

FOREWORD

By Sir DONALD CAMERON OF LOCHIEL, K.T., C.M.G., A.D.C.,
Twenty-fifth Chief of Clan Cameron

I HAVE read the *History of Clan Mackintosh*, so ably written by Mrs. Mackintosh of Mackintosh, with the greatest interest, and have been asked by her to write a Foreword to her work. I do so with some considerable trepidation, seeing that the Clan Cameron, of whom I am Chief, and the Clan Mackintosh waged a long and most bloody war between each other for 360 years. As the reader will learn, this war was all about the ownership of the lands of Loch Arkaig and Glenloy. There seems to be little doubt that Mackintosh was in the right from the point of view of Law and the Camerons right in point of factual possession. Happily this feud ended on 20th September 1665, since when the two Clans have lived most amicably together and for some time past there has been the warmest friendship between the two families. Alfred—more familiarly known as "Alfie"—the twenty-eighth Chief, was a great personal friend of my father's, and I shall never forget all the many kindnesses he showed me ever since I was a boy, and my many visits to Moy Hall are among my happiest recollections; and when he died he did me the honour of appointing me as one of his Trustees. Therefore, whatever may have happened four or five hundred years ago, I now cherish nothing but love and affection for the late Chief of Clan Chattan, and may this friendship between the two families long continue.

The author's account of the long strife between the Mackintoshes and the Camerons is, of course, written from the Mackintosh point of view and, naturally, differs quite considerably from the accounts given in the *Memoirs of Lochiel*, written by Drummond of Balhaldy about 1737 and published in 1842. Who is to say which is correct after all these centuries? But both records agree that peace was eventually established through the intervention of Campbell of Glen Orchy, afterwards the first Lord Breadalbane, who was a cousin germane to both

Chiefs, at the foot of Loch Arkaig, with the River Arkaig and Loch of Arkaig dividing the two Clans. Balhaldy records that peace was signed on 20th September 1665, and that thereafter Lochiel entertained Mackintosh and his Chieftains right royally at his home, which was then at Tor Castle. Curiously enough, the only time Achnacarry is actually mentioned in the *Memoirs of Lochiel* is on this particular historic occasion, and it was not until after this date that Sir Ewen Cameron built a house for himself at Achnacarry and pulled down Tor Castle, which was too close to the garrison at Fort William to be pleasant.

Reading through the two records there is no doubt it was a most disastrous war and exceedingly costly to both sides alike. Nothing was gained by either Chief, and indeed, both lost very heavily. So far as the Camerons were concerned it certainly was an example of the old adage that " Possession is nine points of the Law."

The history of the Mackintoshes and Clan Chattan is, and will be, a most interesting record of old clan history. But what of the future? Will there be any more clan history to write hereafter? The lands of most of the chiefs in the north have, during the last century, been gradually broken up and sold, and the clans all scattered to the four quarters of the globe. The Cluny estates are gone and, with the exception of Moy, the Mackintosh estates are also gone. Very few indeed of the old Highland chiefs possess any territory in the Highlands to-day, for which so much blood was shed during the Middle Ages. *Finis* therefore may now be written to this and all other clan histories; and yet the blood-tie and clan fellowship which unite all clansmen together in a bond of loyalty to their chief and fellow clansmen wherever they may be in the world, are still as strong as ever, of which we have evidence every day from every Highland clan that ever existed. And I feel sure that this latest clan history will be bought and read with avidity by every member of Clan Mackintosh and of the many clans and septs which comprise Clan Chattan, wherever they may be, be it in Australia, Asia or Africa, and Mrs. Mackintosh of Mackintosh is indeed very much to be congratulated on her work.

EXTRACT OF MATRICULATION OF THE ARMS OF MACKINTOSH OF MACKINTOSH-TORCASTLE, CHIEF OF CLAN CHATTAN

Touch not the catt but a glove
Clann Chattan

To All and Sundry whom These Presents Do or May Concern, We, Sir Thomas Innes of Learney, Knight Commander of the Royal Victorian Order, Baron of Learney, Kinnairdy and Yeochrie, Advocate, Lord Lyon King of Arms, Send Greeting; Considering that under the provisions of the Statute 1672 cap 47 & others in that behalf made, We are hereby and in virtue of Our Office of Lyon empowered to Visite the whole Arms borne and used within this Realm, to distinguish them with congruent differences, and to matriculate them in Our Books and Registers, and to give Extracts of All Arms under Our hand & Seal of Office; and Whereas by Petition unto Us of date the 14th day of February last Duncan Alexander Eliott Mackintosh of Mackintosh-Torcastle and Clan Chattan, Inheritor and Representative of the Ancient and Honourable family of the Clan Chattan, Chief or Head of the Clan Chattan, residing at Fairburn, Felixburg, S. Rhodesia, (who was born 1st December 1884, married in the year 1912 Ellen Primrose Smith & has, with other issue, an eldest son and heir-apparent, Kenneth Mackintosh of Clan Chattan younger, born 23rd Nov 1916) shews he is the eldest surviving son, heir-male and representative of the late Alexander Mackintosh (born at Daviot, 27th December 1852) and his wife Anne Lavinia Berkeley, married 24th April 1878; That the said Alexander Mackintosh was the eldest son of Aeneas Mackintosh of Daviot in the County of Inverness and his wife Louisa Fanny Sibella daughter of Major Alexander Macleod; That the said Aeneas Mackintosh of Daviot (born 12th June 1811, died 25th April 1880), immediate younger brother of Alexander Mackintosh of Mackintosh, was the third-born but second surviving son of Angus Mackintosh of Mackintosh, 26th Chief of Clan Chattan and 25th Chief of the Name of Mackintosh, by his wife Archange St Martin: That the said Angus Mackintosh of Mackintosh was heir of tailzie and successor (inter alia under an entail of Sir Aeneas Mackintosh of Mackintosh, Baronet, 23rd Chief of Mackintosh and 24th Chief of Clan Chattan, 2nd August 1819) of Lachlan Mackintosh of that Ilk alias of Torcastle, who was by Declaration 10th September 1672 by Sir Charles Erskine of Cambo, Baronet, Lord Lyon King of Arms, found Chief of the Name of Mackintosh and Chief of the Clan Chattan in respect of his predecessor having anno 1291 married the Heretrix of the Clan Chattan, and in whose name Ensigns Armorial were matriculated in the Public Register of All Arms and Bearings in Scotland, 7th March 1679 as Lachlan Mackintosh of that Ilk, alias of Torcastle: That Alfred Donald Mackintosh of Mackintosh, commonly called The Mackintosh, 29th Chief of Clan Chattan and 28th Chief of Mackintosh, brother and heir of tailzie of Alexander Aeneas Mackintosh of Mackintosh, Chief of Clan Chattan, grandson and heir of entail of the said Angus Mackintosh of Mackintosh, 26th Chief of the Clan Chattan, died 14th November 1938 without surviving male issue, having disentailed the Mackintosh Estates by an Instrument dated 27th February 1877: That the said Alfred Donald Mackintosh of Mackintosh, by Trust Disposition and Settlement of date 4th December 1938 settled upon the Petitioner's first cousin, Rear-Admiral Lachlan Donald Mackintosh, now The Mackintosh of Mackintosh, his Estate of Mackintosh, and along with Moy Hall any articles which should properly belong to "the heir who will succeed to the Mackintosh estates" and to the said mansion house, and inter alia the family seal of arms and armorial standard of The Mackintosh, whereby the said Rear-Admiral as Inheritor of the Mackintosh Estates, along with the said standard and family seal of arms and burial place by succession from his predecessor in the family, became Chief of the Name and Arms of Mackintosh and Head of the Clan Mackintosh, on the principles set forth by Sir George Mackenzie of Rosehaugh, his Majesty's Advocate, in his "Science of Herauldrie": That the said settlement in favour of the Petitioner's cousin, Rear-Admiral The Mackintosh as heir of Tailzie and by tanistry, did not comprehend any settlement expressed in relation to the Chiefship of Clan Chattan, and that Arabella Anne Peace Mackintosh of Mackintosh only grandchild and heir of line of the said Alfred Donald Mackintosh of Mackintosh, having anno 1942 married John Anthony Warre and (as Mrs Warre) become conventionally dead as a Mackintosh, the Petitioner is now the nearest heir of the said Alfred Donald Mackintosh of Mackintosh as aforesaid bearing the name and style of Mackintosh and Torcastle in which the Ensigns Armorial aforesaid are on record in the Public Register of All Arms and Bearings in Scotland, so that the Petitioner is now Inheritor of the Chiefship of Clan Chattan, and Head or Chief of the Clan Chattan, agreably to the Declaration anent the Chiefship of the said "honourable familie of the Clan Chattane" made by the said Lord Lyon Sir Charles Erskine of Cambo, 10th September 1672: That the Ensigns Armorial matriculated as above-mentioned 7th March 1679 in name of the said Lachlan Mackintosh of that Ilk alias of Torcastle were indicative of his position both as Chief of the Name of Mackintosh and Chief of Clan Chattan: That the Petitioner has assumed the name of Mackintosh of Mackintosh-Torcastle and style of Clan Chattan which style of Torcastle was derived from the principal fortalice of the Clan Chattan lands of Glen Lui and Locha Arkaig, Glen Spean and Glen Roy, and was, in a contract with Ewan Cameron of Lochiel 15th June 1664 reserved and borne by sundry successive Chiefs of Clan Chattan by Mackintosh of that Ilk alias of Torcastle That it has transpired from examination of the said armorial standard Chattan is properly Azure, not Sable as recorded during the minority of Lord Lyon Sir Alexander Erskine of Cambo, Azure is consistent with the Declaration by Lord Lyon Sir Charles Erskine of Cambo that the arms awarded to (per fess Or and Azure, a galley of the first) were on account of his being "a cadent of the Laird of Mackintosh's family" Chief of Clan Chattan: and the said Petitioner having prayed that the Ensigns Armorial might be matriculated of new appropriate to him as Chief of the Clan, and with supporters suitable to the Chief of Clan Chattan, and an Interlocutor of date the 25th day of March, finding inter alia, in fact (35) that in consequence of disposal by The Mackintosh Trustees of the of which estate passes down to the heir of the Mackintosh Estates, the arms, Or, a lymphad, sails furled, oars in saltire Azure, flagged derived from or as from Eva, Heritrix of the Clan Chattan (and held by the said Alexander Aeneas Mackintosh of Mackintosh, Captain Donald Mackintosh of Mackintosh, Chief of Clan Chattan, his brother & heir of tailzie) now descendable as inheritance from Eva, Sir George Mackenzie of Rosehaugh, his Majesty's Advocate, states in the 21st chapter of his Treatise, "The Science of Herauldrie" or younger sons do distinguish their arms from those of the principal house or the chief house, as we say in Scotland, are called "distinguish their families from that of their Chief, for so we call the Representative of the family from the French word chef, an the Chief of the Family is called the Head of the Clan," & thus identifies the terms & character "Head of the Clan" in Gaelic with

progress from the said Lachlan at Moy that the galley of Clan 2nd Baronet, which tincture Duncan Macpherson of Cluny viz of Mackintosh as being in his name in the manner having been pronounced by Us Glen Spean Estate whereby no part Gules are the only feudal heritage and Chief of Clan Chattan & Alfred Heretrix of Clan Chattan, (42) that that the marks whereby the cadets brisurs" & further that such brisurs head, & in the Irish, Erse, with us, "Representative of the family in member of the family entitled to the Clan Chattan (who was last

Scots, & both these with proprietorship of the ancestral arms without brisur or mark of cadency, & that the Lords Dunedin, Shaw & Sumner likewise held on 12th December 1921 that the Chief of the Clan is the the undifferenced ancestral arms: Finds in Law (1) That the Petitioner, nearest heir according to the Law of Arms (idem in the name of Mackintosh-Torcastle) of Alfred Donald Mackintosh of Mackintosh, Chief of heir of tailzie by progress in the Glen Spean portion of the Mackintosh Estates from Lachlan Mackintosh of that Ilk, alias of Torcastle, son & heir of William Mackintosh of that Ilk, alias of Torcastle, great-great-great-great-uncle of the said Alfred Donald Mackintosh of Mackintosh is now in right of the Ensigns Armorial as for Mackintosh of Torcastle, matriculated in name of Lachlan Mackintosh of that Ilk, alias of Torcastle, on 7th March 1679 as nearest heir as aforesaid of the last heir of tailzie in possession of the said lands, since there is no tailzie or destination on record or adduced for resettlement of same. (2) That the Petitioner is entitled as of right to matriculate, undifferenced & without brisur or mark of cadency so far as regards the arms of Clan Chattan, the arms matriculated by the said Lachlan Mackintosh of that Ilk, alias of Torcastle, on 7th March 1679, in the manner appropriate to the Representer of the Family of Clan Chattan, but differenced as regards the arms of Mackintosh of that Ilk: (3) That as Inheritor of the Ensigns Armorial of Clan Chattan without brisur or mark of cadency, the Petitioner is subject to reinvestiture of the same in Lyon Register, now Representer, id est Representative, of the Family of Mackintosh-Torcastle, or Clan Chattan. (4) That headship of a Clan is cognisable in the Law of Arms in relation to (a) undifferenced arms, (b) supporters, and (c) name, & is a description relevant & relative to such arms or supporters. (5) That as Inheritor of the arms of Mackintosh-Torcastle or Clan Chattan, without brisur or mark of cadency, the Petitioner, being now "Representer and Chief, for so we call the head of the family" of the Family of Clan Chattan, is accordingly "in the Gaelic head of the Clan" Chattan, as set forth by Sir George Mackenzie of Rosehaugh in his "Science of Herauldrie" (Works, Vol 2, p 618) We do hereby Certify and Declare that We have recognised and recognise the Petitioner under the name & designation of Duncan Alexander Eliott Mackintosh of Mackintosh-Torcastle & Clan Chattan & his son & heir in the name of Kenneth Mackintosh of Clan Chattan younger, & that the Ensigns Armorial appertaining & belonging to the said Duncan Alexander Eliott Mackintosh of Mackintosh-Torcastle & Clan Chattan, Inheritor of the Honourable the Clan Chattan, Head or Chief of the Clan Chattan are matriculated of date April 9th 1947 upon the 36th page of the XXXVIth Volume of Our Public Register of All Arms & Bearings in Scotland, agreably to Our Interlocutor & Warrant of date the 25th day of March last, & are thus blasoned, videlicet - quarterly, 1st, Or, a lion rampant Gules (for MacDuff); 2nd, Argent, a dexter hand couped fessways holding a heart in pale Gules, a label Azure in chief charged with three balls' heads caboshed of the first (for difference) (for Mackintosh); 3rd, Azure, a boar's head couped Or, armed proper, langued Gules, 4th, Or, a lymphad, sails furled, oars in saltire Azure, flagged Gules (for Clan Chattan) over all an inescutcheon en surtout charged as the 4th (for Captain or Chief of the Clan Chattan); above the Shield is placed an Helmet befitting his degree with a Mantling Azure doubled Or & on a Wreath of these Liveries is set for Crest a cat salient proper (for Clan Chattan) & in an Escrol over the same this Motto "TOUCH NOT THE CATT BOT A GLOVE" & on a compartment below the Shield embellished with red whortleberry, being a badge plant of the Clan Chattan, along with this Slughorn "CLANN CHATTAN" are set for Supporters two grey cats salient proper; for his badge a demi-highlandman attired in a helmet proper, & jacket of the tartan of the Chief of Clan Chattan, viz: ½ white: 15 red: 1 black: ½ white: 8 green: ½ white: 1½ yellow: 1½ red: 1 black: 1½ red: 1½ yellow: ½ white: 8 green: ½ white: 1 black: 15 red: ½ white: holding in his dexter hand a Lochaber axe proper, & on his sinister arm a highland targe proper, its boss emblasoned with the arms as on the aforesaid inescutcheon, which badge is depicted upon a standard four yards long with his arms in the hoist, of these Liveries, Or & Azure, along with crest in the second compartment, & a sprig of red whortleberry in the third compartment, & this Slughorn "CLANN CHATTAN" in letters Or upon two transverse bands Gules; & that by demonstration of these Ensigns Armorial he & his successors in the same bearing the name & designation aforesaid or the name Mackintosh of Clan Chattan are amongst all Nobles & in all places of honour to be Accounted, Taken & Received as Chiefs of the Family, Captain or Head of the Honourable the Clan Chattan. In Testimony Whereof We have subscribed this Extract and the Seal of Our Office is affixed hereto at Edinburgh this Ninth day of April in the Eleventh Year of the Reign of Our Sovereign Lord George the Sixth, by the Grace of God, of Great Britain and Ireland and the British Dominions beyond the Seas, KING, Defender of the Faith, Emperor of India, etc, and in the Year of Our Lord One Thousand Nine Hundred and Forty-Seven.

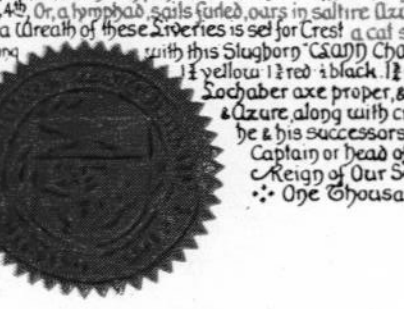

Thomas Innes of Learney
Lyon.

CHAPTER I

MANY legends have arisen around Highland chiefs and their clans, making it very difficult to distinguish fact from fiction in the records that have descended to our time. Highland history can only be traced for about eight hundred years, though many clans claim that their chief holds his land as representative of the first possessor who settled upon the said land much earlier.

It is certain that the clan system prevailed in Scotland from very early days. A clan was like a tribe and the Scots originally were not so much a nation as a race of tribes who made war on each other for the possession of land. A clan is best defined as the grouping together of a number of families all related to each other by blood, under one chief. The clan has been described as "a mixture of tribal tradition clustering round the actual land-holder of the soil" and undoubtedly was a "feudal" system meaning "organisation of the family upon the land." They regarded their chief with great loyalty and devotion, and other neighbouring families of their own volition joined the chief of a powerful clan, with a view to forming an offensive and defensive alliance. They called the hereditary property of the chief the "duthus" or principal estate.

By one account the Mackintoshes are traced with the original Clan Chattan, and are derived from the Dalriadic kings descended from Ferchar Fada, son of Feradach, king of Dalriada, who died in 697. History only starts to emerge clearly after the twelfth century and is not definite until the fifteenth century when charters began to be freely given. The earliest authentic ancestry is traced to Shaw MacDuff, son of the third Earl of Fife, who was of the Royal Family. MacDuff took the name of Mackintosh, "Mac-an-toisich," which means Son of the Chief or Thane. He probably retained in his coat-of-arms the Lion Rampant of the Earls of Fife. In 1163 he came to the north with King Malcolm IV to suppress a rebellion of the men of Moray. As a reward for his services, he was made Keeper of the Royal Castle of Inverness, and received the lands of Petty and Breachley with the forest of Strathdearn in the valley of the Findhorn. The early chiefs are said to have resided in Inverness Castle, but Petty was their early "duthus" and there through centuries the family burial-place has been situated, and is still the resting-place of the Mackintosh chiefs. Shaw Mackintosh, the first Chief of the Clan, died in 1179. All the numbering in this book refers to the chiefs of Mackintosh, except where clearly stated to refer to the chiefs of Clan Chattan.

SHAW, second Chief of Mackintosh, succeeded his father in 1179. He received a confirmation of his father's grants from King William, and was made Chamberlain of the Crown Revenues in his part of the north. Shaw died in 1210.

FERQUHARD, third Chief, succeeded his father and was brought up by his kinsman, Malcolm, Earl of Fife. In an agreement with the Bishop of Moray, Ferquhard is quoted as Seneschal of Badenoch. Ferquhard died in 1240 leaving no son.

SHAW, fourth Chief, was the son of Ferquhard's brother, William, and succeeded in 1240. Shaw acquired Meikle Geddes and the Castle of Rait and, before he became Chief, obtained a lease of Rothiemurchus, in Strathspey, in 1236. The feu-right was not obtained until 1464. He died in 1265.

FERQUHARD, fifth Chief, succeeded his father and lived at Rothiemurchus. He was chosen to lead the Badenoch people against the Norwegians for Alexander III. The MacGillivrays put themselves under the protection of Ferquhard and joined themselves to the Mackintosh clan. Ferquhard was killed in a duel in 1265. After his death, and in the minority of his only son, Angus, the Comyns seized Meikle Geddes, Rait and also the Castle of Inverness. Edward I took the Castle from the Comyns in 1303, but Robert Bruce took it back a few years later. The Mackintoshes did not regain either the Castle, Meikle Geddes or Rait for another hundred years.

ANGUS, sixth Chief, succeeded his father, and was brought up by his uncle, Alexander of Isla. He married in 1291 Eva, the only daughter of Gilpatric or Dougal Dall, Chief of Clan Chattan in Lochaber.

Clan Chattan means Clan of the Cats. There are, however, five theories on the origin of Clan Chattan. One says that they came from the Catti, a tribe of Gauls driven out by the Romans. A second derives it from cat or catai, the name of a weapon. A third says the clan came from Caithness, obtaining its name from the wildcats which infested the district. A fourth says they took their name from Catav, now Sutherland. A fifth theory, which is the most reasonable, says that the clan descended from

Gillichattan Mor, who was " Servant of St. Chattan," and had the galley coat-of-arms. The meaning of " Servant of St. Chattan " is that Gillichattan was the bailie or temporal leader of the Abbacy lands of Ardchattan, and the " duthus " of Gillichattan's race was the estate of Glenloy and Loch Arkaig, where Torcastle was the Chief's seat. It is only certain that the Clan Chattan were found in Lochaber at the close of the thirteenth century. The clan consisted of various families or septs, bearing diverse names, who had banded themselves together under one chief for mutual protection.

Eva was descended from Gillichattan Mor and her father was Gilpatric, or Dougal Dall, sixth in line from Gillichattan Mor.

In 1291 the Chattan chief gave to Angus with his daughter Eva the chiefship of Clan Chattan, and the lands of Glenloy and Loch Arkaig—which lands Mackintoshes held until they were sold to the Camerons in 1666 by the nineteenth Chief of Mackintosh. The chiefship of Clan Chattan was regarded as a heritable honour, and the son-in-law became Chief in right of his wife, just as the husband of a Scottish countess became earl in her right.

On the death of Dougal, Angus Mackintosh succeeded to the lands and chiefship of Clan Chattan, with the approval of the entire clan, and lived at Torcastle. He was the seventh Chief of Clan Chattan, and sixth of Mackintosh. At the death of Angus' uncle, Alexander of Isla, Mackintosh deemed it prudent to withdraw from Lochaber, leaving derelict Eva's lands, and take up his residence at Rothiemurchus. He was followed by the entire Clan Chattan, including the Macphersons, into Badenoch.

It was much later that the feud arose whereby the Macphersons claimed the chiefship of Clan Chattan, and it is convenient here to give the subsequent history of this dispute.

The Macphersons traced themselves back to Kenneth, a male relative of Eva, and claimed that he should have been the chief and his descendants after him. The Macphersons disputed the chiefship of Mackintosh over Clan Chattan, and the feud lasted two hundred years.

Macpherson of Cluny, in 1672, to assert his independence of Mackintosh, applied to the Lyon Office to matriculate his arms as " The Laird of Cluny Macpherson and the only and true representer of the ancient and honourable family of Clan Chattan."

This he obtained, whereupon LACHLAN MACKINTOSH, nineteenth Chief, at once appealed to the Lyon King of Arms, who immediately gave a decree in Mackintosh's favour :

"I, Sir Charles Areskine of Cambo, Knight Baronet, Lord Lyon King of Arms, having perused and seen sufficient evidents and Testimonies from our Histories, my own Registers and Bands of Manrent doe hereby declare, That I find the Laird of M'intosh to be the only undoubted Chieff of the name of M'intosh and to be the Chieff of the Clan Chattan, comprehending the M'Phersones, Mackillvrays, Ferquharsones, M'Quins, M'Faills, M'Baines and others ; and that I have given and will give none of these families any arms but as cadents of the Laird of M'intoshes familie, whose predicessor maried the Heretrix of the Clan Chattan in anno 1291 ; and that in particular I declare, That I have given Duncan M'Phersone of Clunie a coat of arms as a cadent of the forsaid familie. And that this may remaine to posteritie and may be knowen to all concerned, whether of the forsaids names or others, I have subscribed thir presents with my hand at Edinburgh the tenth day of September 1672, and have caused append my seal of office thereto."

Lyon King of Arms at the same time sent the following letter to Clunie :

"Sir, I have given you a coat of arms as a Cadet of M'Intosh his family, and yet you have (upon pretext of that) given yourself out for a chief of the M'Phersons, as we are informed, and have used supporters without any warrant, and given yourself the designation of Chief of the old Clan Chattan ; this is neither fair nor just, and therefore you will be pleased not to abuse any favour I gave you beyond my intention, who is, Sir, your humble Servant.

(Sd. Charles Erskine.)

P.S. I have ordered M'Intosh to keep this letter after you have seen it."

The Lord Lyon gave a fresh grant of arms to Cluny, cancelling that which had contained the words objected to by Mackintosh, viz. "the only and true representer."

Macpherson appears to have disregarded the Lyon's ruling against his assumption of chiefship, for in the next year he enters into a contract of friendship with Lord Macdonell "for himself and taking burden upon him for the heall name of Macphersons and some others called Old Clanchatten as cheefe and principall man thereof." However, he did not claim chiefship of the whole Clan Chattan, but to be chief and representer of the Macphersons and descendants of the Clan Chattan of prehistoric times. In

1724 we find the Chief of the Macphersons signing an agreement in which, in consideration of his receiving from Mackintosh various lands about Loch Laggan, he renounces for all time in favour of Lachlan Mackintosh and his successors all pretension whatsoever he has to the Chieftainry of Clan Chattan, and binds his clan to follow and avow the said Lachlan Mackintosh and his heirs and successors as Chief of the Clan Chattan.

The Clan Chattan in the fourteenth and later centuries was not of the same composition as the prehistoric clan. It was a community consisting of (*a*) descendants of the original clan, (*b*) of Mackintoshes and their offshoots, and (*c*) of families not originally related by blood, such as the MacGillivrays and the M'Queens who voluntarily joined the Clan Chattan. This confederated body is mentioned in history from fourteenth century downwards, and all followed the Mackintosh as Chief.

ANGUS, sixth Chief, had lived for some years at Torcastle on his wife's lands, but removed to Rothiemurchus after Angus Og of Islay succeeded Alexander. Angus Og was unfriendly to Mackintosh and disapproved of his marriage to Eva; however, the Clan Chattan went with Mackintosh. At this time King Robert the Bruce was warring against the Comyns, whom he overthrew at Inverness in 1308. Mackintosh led his men in support of the King and fought at Bannockburn in 1314, where he was the second in the list of chiefs present and one of the chief leaders under Randolph, Earl of Moray, and nephew of the King. Mackintosh was with Moray in the campaign of 1318 in England, and in 1319 was rewarded with a grant of the lands of Benchar, in Badenoch, from which the Comyns had been expelled by Bruce. About this time there took place a large settlement of the Clan Chattan in Badenoch, where Moray was now Mackintosh's feudal superior. After a distinguished career, Angus died in 1345. He was a brave and loyal character, of strong endurance in success and adversity.

CHAPTER II

WILLIAM, seventh Chief (eighth of Clan Chattan), succeeded his father, Angus, in 1345. Before he became Chief he had acquired from the Bishop of Moray, in 1336, the Barony of Moy, which had been reserved for a country seat of the Bishop on account of its beauty, when Shaw, the first Chief, had originally been given the lands of Strathdearn in 1163. In 1336 he also obtained, in his father's lifetime, a right to the lands of Glenloy and Loch Arkaig which John of Isla had claimed under Edward Baliol. A long feud now began with the Camerons who had occupied the lands since Angus, sixth Chief, had left them. As Angus and Eva lived in Badenoch it became difficult for them to retain effectively the possession, as distinct from the right, to the Clan Chattan lands. The Camerons claimed that the lands had been deserted by the Mackintoshes and that they, the Camerons, had been the first to seize and occupy them. William fought and defeated the Camerons at Drumlui. In 1359 William obtained a confirmation by King David II of his rights to Glenloy and Loch Arkaig, but was unable to dislodge the Camerons.

William had fought under David II against England in the second War of Independence. He followed the King into England and was in the battle of Durham, or Neville's Cross, in 1346, where the Scots were totally defeated, the King being captured and the Earl of Moray killed.

In 1347 William obtained a new lease of Rothiemurchus from the Bishop of Moray. He was a man of business and careful to see that his property was secured to his family. He used to spend Christmas at Torchionan, in Loch Arkaig, and desired that he might be buried in the island, since he was determined that, as he could not enjoy his own land in his lifetime, he would have some of it for himself in death. He died at Connage in 1368, and was buried as he wished in the island in Loch Arkaig.

LACHLAN, eighth Chief, succeeded in 1368. He was the eldest son of William, seventh Chief, and was head of the clan for nearly forty years. In his time the feud with the Camerons was hotly pursued by both sides. In 1370 the Camerons, four

hundred strong, made a raid into Badenoch, but when returning home with their booty they were overtaken at Invernahavon by a stronger force of Mackintoshes led by the Chief who had with him the Chiefs of Macpherson and Davidson. Both these chiefs claimed command of the right wing, and when Mackintosh decided in favour of Davidson, the Macphersons took offence and withdrew their men. Mackintosh's numbers were thus much inferior to the Camerons, who totally defeated Mackintosh. On seeing this the Macphersons attacked the Camerons and turned the defeat into a victory.

Far from settling the feud, this battle was followed by such bitter feeling that the Government had to interfere. It was arranged that the Clan Chattan and Clan Cameron should select thirty champions to hold combat in presence of King Robert III at the North Inch at Perth in 1396. It was found that on the Clan Chattan side one champion was missing. A volunteer was found to take his place who was a harness-maker or armourer smith "not great in stature but fierce." He fought bravely and was afterwards adopted into the clan, and the sept of Smith or Gow has survived in Clan Chattan. As a result of the battle the Clan Chattan were successful with eleven survivors, while the Camerons were all slain except one man who leaped into the Tay and escaped. At the battle of the North Inch in 1396, the Mackintoshes were led by Shaw Mackintosh, as Lachlan, the Chief, was too old to fight. As a reward for the victory, Shaw was presented by the Chief with the lands of Rothiemurchus, which Shaw and his descendants occupied. This battle closed the feud for a good many years, but it broke out again in a battle in 1430.

FERQUHARD, ninth Chief, succeeded on the death of his father, Lachlan, in 1407. Ferquhard was a melancholy, indolent and reserved character with no qualities of leadership who was very unpopular as Chief of the Clan. After two years he abdicated and gave up all claims to the succession of his sons, renouncing his birth right in favour of his uncle, Malcolm. He kept only Kyllachy and Corrivory, in Strathdearn, which his family held for two hundred years. Ferquhard's descendants were regarded in the time of Sir Æneas, the twenty-third Chief, as the sixth Cadet branch of the House of Mackintosh ; *i.e.* the heir-male and heir-of-line, having abdicated, remained a member of the clan, but the Chieftain of the Slioch Ferchar vich Lachlan was no longer

the representer of the founder of Clan Mackintosh and of Clan Chattan.

MALCOLM, the tenth Chief, was the son of William, the seventh Chief, who had made a second marriage late in life. He was known as Malcolm Beg, being short and square in build. He was a strong, dominating character whose leadership the clan enthusiastically followed. No doubt Malcolm had exerted powerful influence on Ferquhard to abdicate.

In the year 1411, Donald, Lord of the Isles, claimed and invaded the Earldom of Ross. He then proceeded to invade the Lowlands, with the Islesmen and most of the West Highland clans, and was joined by Mackintosh with the Clan Chattan. On his way southward through Aberdeenshire he was met by the Earl of Mar with an army superior in training if not in numbers. The battle of Harlaw was fought in July 1411, an important battle in Scottish history. Donald was not totally defeated, but the advantage was against him, so that he was obliged to return to the Isles and failed to win the Earldom of Ross. It is said that Donald gave a right to Mackintosh to the lands of Glengarry, but no charter appears until 1446, when there is a grant of the office of bailie of the lands of Glengarry to Duncan, Malcolm's son.

In Malcolm's time the feud with the Comyns flared up again and was finally quenched. In 1424 Alexander Comyn held possession of Meikle Geddes and Rait, which rightly belonged to Mackintosh. Comyn had several Mackintosh men taken and hanged, whose death Malcolm avenged by surprising some of the Comyn's chief men in the Castle of Nairn and putting them to the sword. On this the Comyns invaded his country and advanced to Loch Moy, where they were caught in an ambush and completely routed. Another story says that the Comyns, having driven the Mackintoshes for refuge into the island in Loch Moy, proceeded to dam the loch in order to drown them. A brave Mackintosh went down at dead of night to the dam and bored holes in the boards with which it was lined, placing in each hole a plug with a cord attached. All these cords were fastened to one rope which he finally pulled, releasing the water which rushed out with great force, carrying away the dam and all the army of the Comyns encamped on the bank. The brave clansman, who saved his comrades, was drowned with his enemies.

The Comyns now treacherously offered reconciliation while meditating revenge, and to that end they invited the Mackintoshes to the Castle of Rait to a feast where all animosities should be forgotten. However, one Comyn lad was in love with a Mackintosh lass whom he asked to meet him at the Grey Stone, or listening-stone, near the Church of Croy. There, speaking to the stone in the hearing of his friend, he disclosed to her that a bull's head would be brought in at the feast as a signal for the attack of the Comyns upon the Mackintoshes. The lass warned the Mackintoshes, who thus went to the Castle prepared for action. Immediately the bull's head appeared, each Mackintosh fell upon a Comyn and the whole sept was slaughtered except for the one who communicated the treachery at the Grey Stone. Thus the Mackintoshes regained the Castle of Rait in 1442.

Malcolm lost no time in obtaining a charter for the lands of Meikle Geddes and Rait from Alexander de Seton, Lord of Gordon, in 1442. For a hundred years the Comyns had withheld these lands from the Mackintoshes, until their power was now finally broken.

In 1428 James I visited Inverness and made Malcolm Constable of the Castle, as his forbears had been. The King induced a number of Highland chiefs to meet him there in order to make them responsible for the good behaviour of their clans, but on their arrival he had some executed and others imprisoned. Alexander, Lord of the Isles, and Second Earl of Ross, was put in prison, but when he was released in 1429 he attacked and burned Inverness, though he was unable to take the Castle from Mackintosh. Fearing the approach of a large army against him, Alexander left Inverness. He attempted to entice the Clan Chattan and Clan Cameron, but both these clans supported the King at a battle in Lochaber, where Alexander was heavily defeated. He begged the King to grant him his life, to which the King agreed, but kept him a close prisoner for many years.

Although the Clan Chattan and Clan Cameron both fought for the King against Alexander of the Isles, yet within a year they had a fight which resulted in the almost complete extermination of a sept of the Cameron clan. This fight, which took place in a church on Palm Sunday 1430, is sometimes confused with the account of Invernahavon in 1370.

In 1431 the Earls of Mar and Caithness had an army in Lochaber to restrain the Islesmen, but they were defeated by

Donald Balloch, a cousin of Alexander of the Isles, in a battle at Inverlochy. After his victory, Donald invaded and harried the lands of Clan Chattan and Clan Cameron in revenge for their having supported the royal army against his cousin. Donald was attacked by the King, who compelled him to flee to Ireland. Mackintosh was compensated for the losses he had sustained by a royal grant of Glen Roy and Glen Spean, in Brae Lochaber, which belonged to an uncle of the Lord of the Isles. Mackintosh retained these lands after the death of King James I and obtained confirmation of the grant in 1443.

In time, the Lord of the Isles was liberated and appointed justiciar of the kingdom north of the Forth when he confirmed the grant of Glen Roy and Glen Spean and also gave to Mackintosh the heritable right of Stewardship of the whole of Lochaber. Alexander of the Isles was completely reconciled to Mackintosh, remembering the loyalty of Clan Chattan to his family before 1429 and Malcolm Mackintosh's good service at Harlaw. Encouraged by his favour the Clan Chattan began, in 1441, to invade the Cameron lands, and in a battle at Cailloch Mackintosh's second son, Lachlan, was wounded, and Gillichallum, his fourth son, was killed. This was followed by a raid under Duncan, his eldest son. Finally, Donald Dubh, the Chief of the Camerons, was forced by the animosity of the justiciar to flee to Ireland. He forfeited his lands of Lochiel, which were bestowed on John Garb Maclean.

In 1454 a short feud arose between the Clan Chattan and the Clan Munro, which led to a fight at Clachnaharry. By this time Malcolm was very old, and the quarrel was pursued by his pugnacious grandson, Malcolm Og, son of the Chief's fourth son. This young man heard that the Munroes were passing by Moy on their return from a raid in Perthshire with a large booty of cattle. Malcolm Og demanded from the Munroes a part of the booty as a fee due for their crossing through the Mackintosh country. John Munro offered twenty-four cows and a bull, which Malcolm Og rejected as too little. After this Munro refused to give up any cattle at all and continued on his way home. Malcolm Og summoned his fellow clansmen to pursue Munro and a battle was fought at Clachnaharry. Tradition says that John Munro was killed. Both sides suffered severe loss of life, but the result of the battle is not fully known. A commemoration was erected at Clachnaharry in 1821 bearing the

word Munro on the side facing the shore of Ross, and the words Clan Chattan on the side facing south, with the legend HAS INTER RUPES OSSA CONDUNTUR.

In Malcolm's time several more clans, including the Clan Tearlich or Macleans of Dochgarroch, the Clan Revan or Macqueens, the Clan Andrish and the Clan Chlerich, joined themselves to Clan Chattan.

Malcolm obtained from the Bishop of Moray in 1407 a lease for his life of the Barony of Moy, in Strathdearn, and showed great ability in his long chiefship watching carefully over the interests of his family and clan. Before he fell into the weakness of extreme old age, he was a most vigorous and successful chief, respected by both friends and enemies. He earned favour from King James I, and was bailie of Badenoch, hereditary bailie of Lochaber and Constable of Inverness Castle. He behaved prudently in the quarrel between the Earl of Ross and the King, and pursued his course with tact, courage and ability. He died in 1464, having proved himself one of the greatest chiefs of Clan Chattan.

CHAPTER III

DUNCAN, the eleventh Chief, who succeeded his father in 1464, was the eldest son. Though of a mild and gentle disposition, he led his clan in battle, as we have already seen, and he was a prudent and vigorous chief. Duncan kept himself in favour with the King and also with the Lord of the Isles, obtaining from the latter in 1466 a new charter of the lands of Moymore, Fern, Clunglassen and Stroneroy, also of Achdrom, Glengarry, Letterfinlay and the Leanachans. In 1475 he resigned the lands of Brae Lochaber into the hands of King James III on the forfeiture of the Lord of the Isles, but in 1493 James IV granted Duncan a charter of these lands and confirmed it.

Duncan entered into a band of friendship with Rose of Kilravock and Lord Forbes in 1467, and this was followed by a bond in 1469 promising to refer all disputes to the Earl of Huntly. However, Duncan's brother, Lachlan "Badenoch," would not follow the Chief in this friendship, and with his cousin, Donald Angus Mackintosh, declared that Rose had no right to Kilravock. In 1482 Donald attacked the Castle of Kilravock and did great damage. A royal summons was taken out against Donald in 1498, whereupon he and his family removed into Atholl. They were descended from Angus, third son of the sixth Chief of Mackintosh, and became the Mackintoshes of Dalmunzie.

Duncan disposed of the lands of Rothiemurchus to his cousin, Alistair Mackintosh or Shaw. After some dispute whether Alistair got the liferent only or hereditary possession, it was settled that the Chief and his brother Lachlan renounce for themselves and their heirs for ever all claims of Rothiemurchus in favour of Alistair and his heirs for ever, the rent being "a fir-cone if demanded."

The Chief's son, Ferquhard, caused his father some trouble because of his bold and adventurous disposition. In 1491 Alexander of Lochalsh attempted to regain the Earldom of Ross for his uncle, John of the Isles. Ferquhard joined Alexander against the Chief's wishes, and persuaded a considerable number of Clan Chattan to follow him. Ferquhard stormed and took Inverness Castle, and then with the forces of Lochalsh ravaged the Black Isle of Ross. Then they proceeded to the Mackenzies' country of Strathconan, where they were surprised by the Mackenzies, who completely routed the forces of Lochalsh and the insurrection was quelled. Ferquhard Mackintosh had been joined by Hugh Rose, younger of Kilravock, and the Mackenzies ravaged Ardmanach, of which Hugh Rose was keeper for the Earl of Huntly, then Lieutenant of the North.

Huntly brought the Mackenzies and Mackintosh to trial. Finally the rebellion of Lochalsh ended in the forfeiture of John, Lord of the Isles. Ferquhard Mackintosh and Kenneth Mackenzie were imprisoned by the King in Edinburgh Castle in 1495. Ferquhard remained in prison in Edinburgh, Stirling and Dunbar until the King was slain at Flodden in 1513.

Duncan had taken no part in Ferquhard's rebellious acts and remained in the King's favour. He repaired Inverness Castle and handed over its custody on the King's order in 1495 to Alexander, Lord Gordon. Duncan died in Inverness in 1496, and was buried in the Grey Friars' Church there.

FERQUHARD, the twelfth Chief, succeeded his father in 1495, being at that time in prison. The Clan Chattan was led by his cousin William, eldest son of Lachlan "Badenoch." The Captain of Clan Cameron had given a promise to assist Clan Chattan against all men, but in 1497 Clan Cameron and Clan MacGregor and the Macdonalds of Glencoe raided the Clan Chattan lands of Badenoch and Strathnairn. William subdued the MacGregors first and then routed the Camerons. However, in 1503 the Camerons rebelled against the King and again ravaged Badenoch. The Earl of Huntly called on Clan Chattan to assist him, which they did willingly, as they still claimed the Lochaber lands which were inhabited by the Camerons. However, it took three years before the Cameron insurrection was quelled in 1506, when the Cameron chief was put in prison.

Ferquhard granted a charter in 1505 of all his lands in Lochaber and Brae Lochaber to his cousin William, but subject to restoration by William if Ferquhard should have a lawful male heir. When Ferquhard was released from imprisonment after the death of James IV at Flodden in 1513, William mustered 1800 of Clan Chattan to welcome him at Inverness, and Ferquhard at last took up his position as Chief.

During his captivity the clan had been compelled to assist the King and Huntly under him. However, in the same year of his freedom, his cousin Dougal Mor MacGillichallum, who had helped William to subdue the Camerons, made an unlawful attack on the Ogilvies at Hall Hill, in Petty. He burned the house and chased away the Ogilvies. He was under the displeasure of the Council, but owing to the confusion then prevailing in the kingdom it was not until two years later that he was compelled to make restoration to the Ogilvies.

For over one hundred years, from the accession of Malcolm, seventh Chief, the Clan Chattan had prospered and increased in power. They had successfully reduced their enemies, the Comyns and the Clan Cameron, and had become free of all dependence on the Chiefs of the Isles. Having considerably assisted the King in subduing insurrections, the Clan Chattan had all this time enjoyed royal favour, and were obtaining a leading place among the northern clans. After this time the clan suffered by internal dissensions, and by incurring the enmity of the Gordons, who were Earls of Huntly.

William, thirteenth Chief, succeeded his cousin Ferquhard, who left no legitimate heir, in 1514, having been responsible for many years for leading the clan during Ferquhard's captivity. William had no legitimate son, and his second cousin, John, hoped to become the Chief. John, persuading some of the clan and also his cousins, the Frasers, to follow him, picked a quarrel by demanding the lands of Meikle Geddes. This was refused, but John attacked William at Inverness and murdered him there in 1515. John was pursued by a party under Dougal Mor, and was executed at Glenesk in the same year.

During William's lifetime he succeeded in 1502 to the lands of Gallovie, of which a charter had been granted to his father, Lachlan "Badenoch," by the Earl of Huntly. William acquired Dunachton through his wife and obtained a charter from Huntly for its lands, which were his most important feudal holding. For the next hundred years the Chiefs of Mackintosh were styled "of Dunachton." Soon after the battle of Flodden, William was made co-guardian of Lochaber with the Chief of Clan Cameron, after an insurrection which had for its object to make Donald of Lochalsh Lord of the Isles. William had two natural sons, from one of whom, Donald Glas, descended the Strone branch and the family of Balnespick and Balvraid.

Lachlan, the fourteenth Chief, succeeded his brother in 1515. He was known as Lachlan "Beg," being of small stature, and he was said to be "a verrie honest and wise gentleman, of a peace-loving and law-abiding character." He ruled his clan and followers with prudence and judgment and kept them to their duties. Lachlan sent one hundred men to assist John and Donald Mackay, whose uncle, Neill, was disputing the succession to the chieftainship of their clan. The dispute ended with Neill and both his sons being killed.

In 1520 Lachlan married Jean Gordon, only child of Sir Alexander Gordon of Lochinvar, who is known by Scott's ballad "Young Lochinvar has come out of the West."

Jean Gordon's mother was Jean Kennedy, daughter of Lord Kennedy and sister of the first Earl of Cassilis. This explains the interest shown later by the Earl of Cassilis in the murder of Lachlan's successor by Huntly. Lachlan's marriage with Jean Gordon was arranged by the Earl of Moray, a natural son of James IV, to strengthen his power in the north whilst he was governor of the lands of Glenloy, Loch Arkaig and Glenroy. Lachlan did not succeed to any lands on the death of his wife's father, but added to his armorial bearings a boar's head of the Gordons of Lochinvar. However, he acquired territory in the Aird, which remained in the possession of the Mackintoshes for nearly a century, and with his wife's money bought the lands of Beaufort, Drumchardiny in Kirkhill parish, and the lands of Easter Eskadaile and Kinnairies in Kiltarlity parish. These lands were in a short time sold to Lord Lovat, as they were in the Fraser country, and far off from the Mackintosh's home at Moy.

Lachlan made a bond of friendship with Campbell of Calder and also with Kilravock, Fowlis, Macdonald of Sleat and the Earl of Argyll.

There was a good deal of trouble over the lands of Meikle Geddes and Rait. The earliest acquisition of them by Mackintosh was in the thirteenth century, and the first charter in the Mackintosh muniments is dated 1442. This records that Alexander Seton grants the lands to Malcolm Mackintosh. However, in 1493 we find Alexander Seton gives a charter to William, Thane of Calder, and that the Ogilvies claimed possession, because of the non-entry of the Calders. As the Earl of Huntly had given a charter to Mackintosh in 1488, it is a mystery how Meikle Geddes and Rait should be in question between the Setons and the Calders. In 1521 Lachlan Mackintosh disputed with Campbell of Calder, at which time Calder yielded, and an agreement was signed at Benchar, in Badenoch, that Lachlan should possess the lands for his lifetime.

Dougal Mor, grandson of Malcolm, tenth Chief, who had attacked the Ogilvies in 1513, now seized upon the Castle of Inverness, and he and his sons occupied it for a short time. Dougal, not content with this, in 1520 broke out in mutiny and claimed to be Chief of Clan Chattan, saying that he had done more for the lairdship than any man living. He was then attacked by the Chief, who recaptured Inverness Castle for the King, and Dougal and his sons were killed. In Dougal perished a great warrior.

Lachlan had a nephew, John, who was a natural son of his half-brother Malcolm, and to whom he had given the occupation of Connage. But John was a lawless man and a robber and allied himself with an attendant of the Chief, called Milmoir MacDhaibhidh, who had a grievance against Lachlan. In 1524 John and Milmoir waylaid Lachlan and treacherously murdered him while he was out hunting at Raigmore, for which crime John was imprisoned and later on beheaded at Rothiemurchus.

Lachlan had one legitimate son, William. He also had two natural sons: John, ancestor of a family of Mackintoshes in Dunachton, and William, ancestor of a family in Kinrara and Pittourie.

CHAPTER IV

WILLIAM, the fifteenth Chief, succeeded his father in 1524. As he was a child of three years old, the clan had to choose a leader. The clan chose Hector, the elder of the two natural sons of Ferquhard, the twelfth Chief, as being a man of great courage and bodily strength, though his leadership was not unanimously accepted. The King supported Hector as Captain of Clan Chattan and issued a precept ordering letters of legitimation for both Hector and William.

At this time the Earl of Moray, who was an uncle of the young Chief, took charge of him with the consent of the King. Hector expostulated and tried to regain custody of William peacefully, but the rest of the clan resorted to force, and in 1527 invaded and harried Moray's lands. The strife was so fierce that a royal order of extermination was issued against Clan Chattan. Hector was clever enough not to be implicated, and the Earl of Moray did not carry out the order to exterminate the Mackintoshes, as the order had sufficient effect to deter their invasion. Hector gave a promise of allegiance to Lord Moray in 1530, but broke this bond and made war on Moray and the Ogilvies in the next year. With his brother William he invaded Moray's country and laid siege to Darnaway Castle, which he failed to capture. He then fell upon the unfortunate Ogilvies at Hal Hill, in Petty, where he was victorious, but failed to capture the young Chief, who had been sent south to the Earl of Cassilis.

Lord Moray marched against Hector's forces, taking three hundred prisoners, including Hector's brother William. Hector himself escaped but William was hanged and many of the prisoners were executed. Lord Moray held a court at Tordarroch to try all who were concerned in the rising and to question them as to the whereabouts of Hector, which none would disclose. Very little more is known of Hector, who later gave himself up to the King and received the Royal pardon in 1532. He had no further power and was probably assassinated by a monk in St. Andrews.

WILLIAM, the fifteenth Chief, took up his position as leader of the clan in 1540 at the age of nineteen. He is described as

" a gentleman of fine qualities and much distinguished for his spirit and politeness, and a perfect pattern of virtue."

In his early days the Earl of Moray strengthened William's position as Chief, but on the death of Moray the Earl of Huntly became Lieutenant of the North. From Huntly William obtained in 1543 a liferent of Benchar, Clune, Essich and Schiphin, including Coignafearn and the five Coigs, at the head of the Findhorn. Some of the principal members of Clan Chattan bound themselves to renounce their dependence on William if he should break his bond of allegiance to Huntly.

In 1544 Huntly called upon Mackintosh to bring the Clan Chattan to help him settle a feud between two rival claimants of the chiefship of Clan Ranald. Huntly supported Ranald, the legal claimant, against John Moydertach, who, although illegitimate, had a strong following. Mackintosh followed Huntly with a force of 1500 men and Huntly also called up the Frasers and the Grants. They marched upon the insurgents, who retired, and Huntly, without a battle, replaced Ranald as Chief. Huntly then withdrew, but Mackintosh offered his continued support to Lord Lovat and the Frasers. This was unfortunately refused, and the Mackintoshes and Grants parted with the Frasers and Ranald. John Moydertach waylaid the Frasers at Kinloch Lochy where there was a great slaughter, and Lord Lovat and his son and Ranald were all killed. Some of the Clan Chattan were waylaid and killed at Abertarff. The Chief avenged this by making an expedition into Glengarry to harry the Clan Ranald. However, John Moydertach succeeded in establishing himself as Chief of his clan and proceeded to defy the authority of the King, whereupon he and his allies, Donald of the Isles, the Captain of Clan Cameron, and Macdonald of Keppoch were denounced for treason. Mackintosh, as Deputy Lieutenant of the North, captured Lochiel and Macdonald of Keppoch and sent them to Huntly, who beheaded them. John Moydertach obtained a pardon in 1548.

In 1545 William obtained from the Bishop of Moray a new right to the barony of Moy, because the old Charters were decayed through age. Moy had long been occupied as the headquarters of the Mackintoshes, and there are among the Mackintosh Writs four documents relating to this matter. The first is a charter by the Bishop in April 1545 granting " in feu ferme to William Mackintosh of Dunachton and Captain of

Clan Chattan the lands of Moymore, Moybeg, Altnaslanach, Tullochclury, Sleauch, Dalmagarry with mill and kiln thereof, Ruthven and Innerin a with their pertinents in the barony of Moymore, and Ardclauch and the regality of Spynie. Mackintosh to pay a nominal rent to the Bishop and his successors, to give personal attendance at the Bishop's courts and also to give military service when required in the Queen's army."

Huntly was made Earl of Moray in 1548, with the lordships of Abernethy, Petty, Breachley and Strathdearn, and thus became the feudal superior of the Chief of Clan Chattan. Huntly had been jealous of the late Earl of Moray in his lifetime and had resented the favour Moray showed to Mackintosh. Huntly found that Mackintosh was able to command a greater following in the north than his own and was very popular with all his neighbours, whereas he (now Earl of Moray) was most unpopular. Huntly endeavoured to get Mackintosh to give him a further bond to support him in all his undertakings, but this Mackintosh refused to do, and Huntly resolved to crush him. Huntly deprived Mackintosh of his deputy lieutenancy and persecuted him in petty ways.

William Mackintosh had an enemy of his own clan in his cousin Lachlan, son of the man who murdered William's father. Lachlan went to Huntly and accused William of conspiring to murder the Earl. This was readily believed, and Huntly seized Mackintosh treacherously in 1550 and took him to Aberdeen, where he arranged a public trial with himself as judge. The charge was impossible to disprove, as the Court House was "packed" entirely with Huntly's supporters. Huntly declared the whole of Mackintosh's estate forfeit, and sentenced Mackintosh to be beheaded. The sentence would probably have been carried out there and then but for the courageous conduct of the Provost of Aberdeen, Thomas Menzies, who protested against the unfair nature of the trial, and finding his protests unavailing, left the court and publicly appealed to Parliament.

Huntly disregarded this protest as he was high in the favour of the Queen Regent, and considered his power too great for him to fear Parliament. He was preparing to put the death sentence into execution when the doughty Provost summoned the citizens in arms to arrest the crime. Unfortunately they could not rescue Mackintosh from his captors, as the Earl had carried off William to his own castle of Strathbogie. There, young Mackintosh was completely at the Earl's mercy and was never seen again.

The mystery surrounding Mackintosh's fate gave rise to numerous stories, and Sir Walter Scott gives the most popular one in his *Tales of a Grandfather*. According to Scott, William escaped and became a fugitive, but finding his situation desperate and his clan in danger of extermination, returned to Huntly's castle and throwing himself on Lady Huntly's mercy, prayed that Huntly's vengeance might fall on him and not on his clan.

Lady Huntly received him in the kitchen at Bog-of-Gight. " Mackintosh," she said sternly, " you have offended the Gordon so deeply that he has sworn by his father's soul that he will never pardon you till he has brought your neck to the block."

" I will stoop to even that humiliation to secure the safety of my father's house," replied the young Chief, and undoing the collar of his doublet he knelt down and laid his neck on the rough block on which sheep and cattle were cut up for domestic use. He doubtless believed that in so doing he was merely making an act of homage and submission to the Gordon, but at a sign from the Countess the cook stepped forward and raising his heavy cleaver struck the unfortunate young man's head from his body.

Huntly himself was absent with the Queen Regent in France when this black deed was done, but the Clan Chattan bitterly resented the crime of the execution of their Chief by his instigation. They could not proceed against Huntly, whose power was too great, but they attacked the traitor Lachlan who had accused William, and Lachlan was slain in his house at Connage in 1551. All Lachlan's followers were forced to leave the country in the same year.

In 1552 Huntly granted all the lands of William Mackintosh to Alexander Lord Gordon, his eldest son. These included Glenroy, Glenspean, Glenloy and Loch Arkaig, also Drumchardiny, Incolme, Cragaig, Kinnairies, Eskadaile and Ardellan in the Aird. He also made him tenant of Moymore, Moybeg and other lands in Strathdearn under the Bishop of Moray.

In 1554 Huntly was sent by the Queen Regent on an expedition against John Moydertach and the Clan Ranald, but he failed because his Lowland troops feared to go into Lochaber, and as his Clan Chattan vassals hated him he had only a few Highlanders available. When he abandoned his enterprise the

Queen Regent was much displeased, and committed him to Edinburgh Castle pending an inquiry into his actions. All his enemies now brought accusations against him as the "pryme author of all these troubles in the Northe, and that for the beheading of the Lairde of Mackintoche." The Earl of Huntly was deprived of the Lordship of Abernethy and the Earldom of Moray and to be banished for five years. The Queen altered the sentence of banishment to a fine of £5000 and restored him to the office of Chancellor.

In 1557 the Earl of Cassilis summoned the Earl of Huntly and his son, Lord Gordon, to appear before Parliament to hear the sentence of the forfeiture of Mackintosh's lands dating from 1550, "reduced, rescinded and annulled." The Parliament also declared the death sentence illegal. William Mackintosh left one surviving son, Lachlan.

CHAPTER V

LACHLAN, the sixteenth Chief, succeeded his father in 1550 at the age of seven, and the clan chose Donald Mackintosh, great-grandson of Malcolm Beg, tenth Chief, and ancestor of the Kyllachy family, to act as Tutor. Lachlan, known as Mor, was well brought up by Kenneth Mackenzie of Kintail at Eilandonan, and afterwards married Kenneth's daughter. He was a staunch Protestant.

In 1562 he was attached to the Court of Mary Queen of Scots. The Queen proposed to give her brother James the Earldom of Moray, and thus to conciliate the Protestant Party, whose leader he was. The Earl of Huntly, who held this title, was a Roman Catholic. He was deeply offended and marched against the royal forces. Queen Mary arrived at Inverness Castle, where she was refused admittance by Alexander Gordon, who held it for Huntly. Lachlan Mackintosh summoned the Clan Chattan, who came with the Munroes and Frasers and others to the help of the Queen and took the Castle. The royal army proceeded to Aberdeen, where James was made Earl of Moray and the Earl of Huntly was outlawed. In 1562 there was a battle at Corrichie, in which the Mackintoshes were part of the royal army, where Huntly was defeated and killed.

In 1567 Mary was forced to abdicate, but she still had a party in Scotland, of which the new Earl of Huntly was leader. In 1568 Lachlan Mackintosh was reconciled to Huntly, and probably fought under him at Langside where the Queen's supporters were defeated by Moray. In this year Huntly gave Mackintosh a new charter of the lands of Bendochar, Clune, Kincraig, Schethin, Essich, Bunchrubin, Duntelchaig and Tordarroch. These lands were to go to James McConil Glas, in case of Lachlan having no lawful heirs-male. Lachlan gave a bond of allegiance to Huntly and also gave the Earl the disposition of his lands of Rothiemurchus. This property had belonged to the Mackintoshes for three hundred years, but since 1539 it had passed to the Gordons, which was a grievance of the Mackintoshes. Huntly sold Rothiemurchus to the Grants in 1567, but in 1568 Huntly gave Lachlan a new charter of the Dunachton and Loch Laggan lands, and signed a contract to

Lachlan Mackintosh for the whole of the lands of Rothiemurchus. This contract was not fulfilled, for Grant was not prepared to give up Rothiemurchus. He refused Mackintosh's offer to buy it back and disregarded a personal appeal by Mackintosh, who called Rothiemurchus his own native country. Mackintosh was now infuriated and he and his clan did all they could to harass the Grants, both there and elsewhere.

In 1568 Lachlan gave to James M'Conil Glas a wadset of all the lands in Huntly's charter and also of Dunachton, Dalnavert, Kinrara-na-Choille, Gallovie, Kinlochlaggan, Muckoull and part of Pittowrie, and the barony of Moy in Strathdearn. This wadset was redeemable by Lachlan or his heirs on payment of a rose noble in the parish church of Inverness. James was the son of Donald Glas, a natural son of the thirteenth Chief.

In 1569 Huntly, Mackintosh and other chiefs gave a bond of submission to the Regent Moray for King James VI. The next year the Earl of Moray died, and Huntly no longer held to his bond, but rejoined the Queen's faction. Mackintosh therefore had a breach with Huntly, but the Macphersons mutinied and broke away from the Clan Chattan. In 1571 Mackintosh was granted the lands of Ardersier and Delnies, which led to trouble with Campbell of Calder and Robert Lesley, both of whom also desired the lands, and Lesley had in fact been placed there by the Bishop of Ross. Calder persuaded Lesley to sell Ardersier to him, whereupon the Mackintoshes raided Calder and a feud raged for several years. In 1581 Mackintosh was going near Cawdor Castle with only nine men, when Calder waylaid him with twenty horse and forty foot. Calder rode forward but his horse being shot he was thrown and struck his head against a block of ice. Some of the Mackintoshes ran to kill him, but their Chief interposed and spared his life. This forbearance so impressed Calder that he made peace with Mackintosh, which continued throughout their lives.

Since 1568 Mackintosh had harassed the Grants at Rothiemurchus, but now arbiters were brought into the dispute and he was prevailed upon to end the feud. In 1586 Mackintosh finally renounced all claim to the lands of Rothiemurchus, he and Grant promising to help each other to hold safely their respective lands.

In 1588 the Clan Chattan followed the Earl of Sutherland in his warfare against the Earl of Caithness. This did not last long, but the Clan Chattan were next called out against the Clan Gregor who had murdered the King's forester and were under royal orders of extermination. Then the Mackintoshes joined the Earl of Moray in protecting the Grants against the Earl of Huntly, and Huntly induced the Macphersons of Badenoch to leave Mackintosh and follow him. Huntly pursued Moray to Donibristle, by the Forth, and obtained a commission to bring Moray to trial in Edinburgh. Moray attempted to escape, but was followed and killed. Huntly, dreading the Protestant fury in Edinburgh, returned to the north, where he found the Mackintoshes and Grants had invaded his home country, laying waste Glenbucket and Abergeldie, and plundering Strathavon, Glenlivet and Strathdon. In 1592 there was a commission against Huntly and the Earl of Atholl with Lord Lovat, so Mackintosh and many others advanced against him to take vengeance for the death of the Earl of Moray. However, the King sent up the Earl of Angus to cause all parties to sign an assurance of truce. This was done, but Cameron of Lochiel fell upon the Clan Chattan and slew a great number, for which the Mackintoshes held Huntly responsible. They seized Huntly's rents in Badenoch and those of the castle lands of Inverness and also laid waste the Cameron lands in Lochaber. Mackintosh gathered seven clans, and slew as many of Huntly's followers as he could find.

In 1593 Huntly wrote and complained to the King of the breaking of the truce, whereupon James VI granted a dispensation of the Act of Intercommuning made against Huntly, in consideration of the damage and slaughter wrought by the Clan Chattan and others in Huntly's lands. Immediately after obtaining the dispensation Huntly invaded Petty and laid waste the land and slew two hundred inhabitants. On his return he found that the Mackintoshes had raided Strathbogie with great slaughter. He pursued the Mackintoshes, and after a severe fight Huntly was victorious.

The Chief of the Clan Chattan, who was at this time Captain of the Castle of Inverness, made a bond of friendship with the Earl of Argyll against Huntly. The Protestant Ministers accused the Earls of Huntly, Errol and Angus of conspiring with the King of Spain to restore the Roman Catholic religion in Scotland, and obtained sentence of forfeiture against the Earls, who took up arms in their own defence. Huntly was followed by the

Camerons and Clan Ranald and by such Macphersons as he had detached from Clan Chattan.

Argyll took the field with five thousand men, including the Clan Chattan and the Grants, but was defeated at Glenlivet, although the Clan Chattan and Macleans repulsed the Camerons. When the news of the defeat was brought to Parliament the Ministers were furious and induced the King, in spite of his partiality for Huntly, to proceed in force to the north to reduce the rebels. Huntly and Erroll left the country and their castles were demolished. The Duke of Lennox was made Lieutenant of the North, and was charged with restoring quiet and order. He made the Chief of Clan Chattan Justice Depute to assist him.

Huntly was soon recalled from banishment, and the King restored him his estates and made him Marquis of Huntly. At Aberdeen, in 1597, Huntly and Erroll formally renounced papistry and, adopting the Protestant religion, were released from excommunication. At the same time Huntly was reconciled to his old enemies, Lord Forbes and Irvine of Drum, and the next month to the Chief of Mackintosh.

At this time the Mackintoshes of Gask, who were Huntly's largest tenants in Badenoch, gave a bond of allegiance to the Chief of Clan Chattan, which included several of the Farquharsons, Mackintosh of Dalmunzie and M'Colme of Glensche.

Lachlan Mackintosh was a great Protestant and encouraged the Presbyterian ministers to instruct all his tenants and largely provided their stipends at his own expense. He renounced the already hopeless cause of Queen Mary after her flight into England in 1569. Lachlan had trouble with his sons, who did not uphold their father's reconciliation with Campbell of Calder, and more especially after his eldest son's widow married Donald Campbell. Malcolm and William Mackintosh twice raided Calder's lands and disputed their sister-in-law and her husband's life-rent for Dunachton. Calder's sons were brought as prisoners to the Chief at Culloden, who at once released them. He was very much displeased with his sons, whom he refused to see for a year. William was put in prison and the Clan Mackintosh had to pay a considerable fine as a penalty to the Crown. Lachlan invaded the Cameron country and compelled the Camerons to pay a rent of 80 merks for Glenloy and Loch Arkaig, and to give him allegiance. In return the Camerons attempted to attack him, but, as their Chief was a minor, were too much divided among themselves. In 1598 there was an agreement that Allan Cameron of Lochiel should hold a wadset of half the lands, on payment of 6000 merks, and hold the other half on promising service to Mackintosh.

In 1606 Lachlan Mackintosh died and was the first Chief to be buried at Petty, which became the hereditary burial-place of the chiefs of Clan Chattan. During Lachlan's lifetime he had witnessed the dethronement of Queen Mary and her imprisonment and execution, the Reformation of Scotland, and the Union of England and Scotland under one sovereign, events in which he and his clan had been more or less directly concerned. Lachlan acquired the Crown lands of Culloden and also Tullich, Elrig, and Lairgs in Strathnairn and entered into many bonds and engagements. His lands were a good deal wasted in war, he had heavy expense in buying out his daughter-in-law's life-rent in Dunachton, Kinrara and Dalnavert in Badenoch, Duntelchaig and Bochrubin in Strathnairn and Glenroy in Brae Lochaber, and to meet his liabilities he was obliged to borrow largely by bond and wadset, which greatly embarrassed his two successors, and in the end helped to reduce the family estate.

CHAPTER VI

LACHLAN, the seventeenth Chief, at the age of thirteen, succeeded his grandfather in 1606. In his minority his uncle, William Mackintosh of Benchar, led the clan. At first Lachlan was looked after by Sir John Campbell of Calder, but King James VI sent for him to England in 1608 and made him a Gentleman of the Bedchamber.

The first object of William of Benchar was to reunite the clan, and especially to reconcile the Macphersons, who had been first beguiled by Huntly and afterwards neglected by him. William called for a Bond of Union in 1609, and summoned the whole of Clan Chattan to meet him at Termit, in Petty. There was a great response and a huge gathering assembled. This was a clan Parliament and a giving of homage to the Chief. The heads of the Macpherson families of Cluny, Invereshie and Pitmean, with others of Clan Muirich, came from Badenoch; the Macqueens, Macbeans, and Mackintoshes from Strathdearn; the MacGillivrays from Stratherrick; the Macphails and also the Farquharsons. They met their brother clansmen of Strathnairn, Petty and Inverness, for the purpose of peaceably ending all their quarrels, and of swearing a firm friendship for the future under Mackintosh, as their "Captain and Chief." In the words of the Bond: "Wherethrough that perpetual amity, friendship and kindness may remain and abide betwixt them and their chief in times coming, and amongst the whole kin of Clan Chattan." They accepted William as leader during the minority of Lachlan. William signed the Bond, as did his three brothers, Malcolm, John and Duncan, all surviving sons of the late Chief. Macpherson of Cluny signed, also two more Macphersons, and all those who could write. There were a large number who could not, but their hands were guided by the Notary. By this Bond of Union the power of the Clan Chattan was firmly established in a prosperous and settled condition.

Lachlan Mackintosh left the Court in 1610 and arrived among his clansmen to take up his position as Chief. He was a very tall man and is described as having "a sweet and benevolent temper." His first troubles were caused by the Earl of Enzie, son of the Marquis of Huntly, who demanded that Mackintosh should call out the Clan Chattan against Cameron of Lochiel. The Camerons had made an agreement with the Earl of Argyll to become vassals of Argyll for the lands of Lochiel. Mackintosh refused to assist Enzie, who proceeded against Lochiel without him, and forced Lochiel to become his vassal. The Earl of Moray, who was Enzie's brother-in-law, was angry with Mackintosh and took notice of a quarrel between a Moray and the Chief, when the latter won a horse race he rode at Nairn. Moray ordered those of Clan Chattan living on his lands to follow Enzie in spite of their Chief, and sent a messenger to inform Mackintosh. This enraged the Chief so much that he gave the messenger a beating. Moray, as Lieutenant in the North, treated this as an act of contempt of court and put Mackintosh in prison in Edinburgh. As he was in the King's favour, Mackintosh was soon released and returned to the north.

In 1616 Mackintosh gave notice to Lochiel that he was about to proceed to Inverlochy to hold courts as heritable Steward of Lochaber. Lochiel assembled two hundred men and attacked Mackintosh at the fords of the Lochy and prevented his passage. Mackintosh reported Lochiel to the Privy Council and obtained a decree of removal of him and his clan from Glenloy and Loch Arkaig and a forfeiture of their tenancy. Lochiel and his party disobeyed an order to appear before the Privy Council.

In 1617 Lachan Mackintosh was knighted by the King. Sir Lachlan entered Lochaber with a large force and compelled Lochiel to come to terms, signing a truce and agreeing to give up the lands; but as Lochiel failed to do so, Sir Lachlan again appealed to the law, and Lochiel's son, John, was put in prison, "as a pledge for his father's obedience." Lochiel still continued in possession.

Sir Lachlan was commissioned to proceed against MacRanald of Keppoch, who had rebelled with Macdonald of Isla against the Government. Mackintosh was unsuccessful, as also was Enzie, who attempted to subdue and capture Keppoch. In 1618 Mackintosh tried again, and in order to raise a larger force he called to all his clansmen, including those dwelling on Enzie's lands, to join him. Enzie resented this strongly and caused Mackintosh's commission against Keppoch to be cancelled. Enzie attempted to evict Mackintosh's men from Benchar, but failing in this, he claimed the tithes of Culloden, and forbade Mackintosh to collect them. When Mackintosh drove away

Enzie's messengers from Culloden, Enzie appealed to the Privy Council and had Sir Lachlan outlawed. Sir Lachlan went to England to appeal to the Court, and during his absence Enzie tried to enter Culloden, but was prevented by Sir Lachlan's uncle. Lord Lovat acted as mediator and persuaded Enzie to depart without bloodshed.

Lord Enzie then went to London himself to complain, and in spite of Mackintosh's favour at Court, the Chief was given a term of imprisonment in Edinburgh Castle.

In 1622 Sir Lachlan was again in London at Court. He was in great favour with the King, who gave him a promise that he should be Earl of Orkney. The Prince of Wales, later Charles I, gave Sir Lachlan a sword, which he took from his own side as a parting gift. This sword is preserved to this day as an heirloom at Moy, and is always carried on the coffin at the funerals of the Chiefs. The King now gave Mackintosh a letter to prosecute Lochiel with fire and sword, and ordering the Council to give Sir Lachlan full commission to call out the Clan Chattan and whoever he required to assist him. The letter also ordered Lord Huntly and his son to aid Sir Lachlan's efforts. The Chief set out immediately for the north, but he only reached Gartenbeg, in Strathspey. In obtaining the support of twenty-two other chiefs and gentlemen, he probably over-exerted himself, dying suddenly at Gartenbeg at the age of twenty-nine.

Sir Lachlan had incurred considerable debts and was obliged to sell to the Frasers the lands of Beaufort, with Drumchardiny, Holm, Rhinduie, Cragaich, Eskadaile and Kinnairies. He also owed large sums to his father-in-law, Grant of Freuchie.

WILLIAM, the eighteenth Chief, at the age of nine, succeeded his father in 1622. For the fourth time in succession the clan were at the disadvantage of a long minority, and were the more unfortunate in that the next Sir John Grant took charge of affairs. He was William's maternal uncle, and the clan objected to his conduct, no doubt because Grant was not of the Clan Chattan.

The Earl of Moray, who was now allied with Huntly, pursued his feud with the Clan Chattan, forgetting their previous loyalty to his house, and demanded the withdrawal of the Mackintoshes from Petty. The Mackintoshes obeyed, but five hundred of them, under Lachlan, afterwards of Corrybrough, and Lachlan of Kyllachy, attacked Castle Stuart in 1624. They harried the surrounding district and yet refrained from shedding innocent blood. The Earl of Moray declared them rebels and outlaws. Moray was made Lieutenant in the North, and this title gave offence to Huntly, his father-in-law. A breach took place between the two nobles, and in consequence Moray was reconciled to the Mackintoshes and restored them in Petty. Huntly succeeded in ousting his son-in-law from his post as Lieutenant and in bribing some of the Macphersons to break away once more from Clan Chattan.

William took up his position as Chief in 1634. He took legal action against his uncle and tutor, Sir John Grant of Freuchie, who was ordered to pay William £834. Grant had also granted a wadset of the lands of Glenloy and Loch Arkaig to Lochiel which Mackintosh redeemed in 1637, but as usual the Camerons refused to give up the lands. William was much harassed by the debts of his father, and in 1637 he sold Culloden to Duncan Forbes for about £1084.

The remainder of William's chiefship coincided with the Civil War, in which his clan took part, although William had not a strong enough constitution to undertake active service himself. William was loyal to the King, and many of the Mackintoshes, Macphersons and Farquharsons fought under Huntly and Montrose. They sent men to the field for Kings Charles I and II and for King James VII.

The Earl of Argyll made himself the head of the Covenant party against King Charles I. In 1644 Mackintosh was made Lieutenant in the county of Moray and was ordered to follow Montrose against Argyll. James Mackintosh of Strone accordingly led a force of Clan Chattan and the Macdonalds of Keppoch, the Macphersons joining Montrose separately under Ewen of Cluny. The Farquharsons had already been out against Argyll in the Trot of Turriff in 1639, and they now followed Huntly. The King's fortunes went up and down until he was imprisoned and executed in 1649. Mackintosh had been appointed governor of Inverlochy Castle in 1648, but he was deprived of this post by Argyll in 1649, and the ill-fated Montrose was hanged in Edinburgh.

In 1650 Cromwell was in power and advanced into Scotland, where Charles II had been proclaimed King and received by all parties, including the Marquis of Argyll. Charles, on his defeat by Cromwell at the Battle of Dunbar in 1650, appealed to Mackintosh for help, but the Clan Chattan had been split up under different leaders and William was unable to give much assistance. Charles was decisively defeated at Worcester in 1651, but three parties of Clan Chattan fought in 1652 under Lord Glencairn at Loch Garry, where they were heavily defeated. The force included Farquharsons and Mackintoshes from Badenoch, Strathdearn and Strathnairn. During the whole period of the Commonwealth the Clan Chattan remained faithful to the King. The Macphersons followed the war under Huntly, cutting themselves off from Clan Chattan, breaking the Bond of Union of 1609 and asserting their independence. William had a lawsuit with Cameron of Lochiel for the lands of Glenloy, and Loch Arkaig and obtained rent from Lochiel for some years in arrears. General Monk, Cromwell's representative in Scotland, tried to reconcile the disputers, but without success.

William died in 1660, having seen the monarchy restored in Charles II. He was " a man distinguished for piety, just and equitable in his conduct, faithful to his word, of dignified behaviour and good manners. He cultivated friendship with constancy and care, and though his body was weak and sickly, his mind was truly great."

CHAPTER VII

LACHLAN, the nineteenth Chief, succeeding his father in 1660, was faced with a crisis in the dispute with the Camerons over Glenloy and Loch Arkaig. These lands were said to have come to the Mackintoshes in 1291, when the sixth Chief married the heiress of Clan Chattan. The Camerons lived there in the Mackintoshes' absence, but the seventh Chief of Mackintosh claimed the lands back again and obtained a charter of them in 1337. As the Camerons refused to give them up, Mackintosh tried to eject them by force, and thus began the feud.

During the sixteenth century, Mackintosh writs relating to the lands are found as belonging to Mackintosh, but being in ward of the King through non-entry. However, to be fair to the Camerons, there is a charter from the King, dated 1527, for the lands of Glenloy and Loch Arkaig and of Brae Lochaber " in fee and heritage forever " to Ewen Allanson, the Cameron Chief. The next record is a Crown precept in 1545 in favour of William Mackintosh, fifteenth Chief. Arrangements were made in 1569 and 1598. Then in 1616 Lochiel was sentenced to forfeit his lands and move out of them, giving them up to Mackintosh, but this sentence had no effect. In 1622 Sir Lachlan Mackintosh obtained a commission against Lochiel, but still Lochiel remained in possession. The matter came up again in 1635 and 1637, but no one could actually displace Lochiel.

A lawsuit was brought by William Mackintosh in 1660, and was carried on by his son Lachlan. In 1661 Lachlan petitioned Parliament to force Lochiel to give up the lands in favour of Mackintosh, " considering that he is impoverished and that Lochiel has kept him out of property and money for many years." An Act was passed ordering Lochiel to repossess Mackintosh, but a delay occurred owing to the King intervening. King Charles II proposed to settle the dispute by compromise, and he gave Lochiel an interview at which he said that though he would not interfere with the law, yet that neither Lochiel's life nor his estate should be in danger. The King feared that strife would break out and he wrote to the Privy Council to settle the matter without peace being disturbed.

In 1662 Mackintosh obtained from the Privy Council a decree

against Lochiel and his clan, ordering them to remove from the disputed lands and asking for a commission of fire and sword to enforce the decree. As this was refused, in 1663 Mackintosh petitioned again, and this time was successful. A long list of Commissioners was issued for pursuing Lochiel with fire and sword to remove him from Glenloy and Loch Arkaig, and to take him and his tenants as rebels and traitors. All the leading gentlemen in the four counties of Inverness, Ross, Nairn and Perth were charged to assist the Clan Chattan.

Lachlan Mackintosh now attempted to call up all the forces to which the Commission entitled him, but he was bitterly disappointed to find that one friend after another failed him, and even his own clansmen were prevented by their landlords from attending their Chief. The Macphersons held aloof, and Lochiel had intrigued with many Mackintoshes, who now refused to rally. Finally, Mackintosh assembled a force of five hundred men at Inverness, on the east side of the river Ness. Lochiel mustered three hundred men on the west side. No fighting took place, however, as the Bishop of Moray and Cumming of Altyre arrived as mediators between the two clans. They succeeded in arranging an agreement by which Mackintosh sold the lands of Glenloy and Loch Arkaig to Lochiel for £40,000. It was soon proved that Lochiel could not produce the money, and Mackintosh resolved to attack him later on.

Mackintosh now attempted to reunite his clan, and in 1664 a Bond of Union was signed by most of the leading men of Clan Chattan binding themselves to follow Lachlan as Chief and to support his commission against Cameron of Lochiel. Cluny did not sign, but other Macphersons did, although they raised various conditions, as did the Mackintoshes of Connage and Kyllachy.

After many delays and conferences with the Privy Council, it was proposed that Lochiel should pay Mackintosh seventy-two thousand merks—which infuriated Mackintosh, who called it "a naughty inconsiderate rate!" Mackintosh again assembled his clan, including Cluny and other Macphersons, Farquharsons, Grants, Forbeses and Macdonalds. Mackintosh marched down the north side of Loch Lochy and encamped at Clunes, on the north side of Loch Arkaig, with 1500 men—Lochiel encamped at Achnacarry with 1200 men—and he sent Cameron of Erracht to make a feint attack from the small island at the foot of Loch

Arkaig. Lochiel with his main force prepared to march round the head of Loch Arkaig to attack the Mackintoshes on the flank—at that point Breadalbane arrived with 300 men to insist on peace. He was first cousin to both Chiefs, and he said that whoever refused to make peace he would join up with the other side and attack. This brought the desired result, and peace was signed on 20th September 1665, and Lochiel entertained Mackintosh and Breadalbane and all the chieftains at his house that day. The terms offered were as before, that Lochiel should buy his lands from Mackintosh for seventy-two thousand merks (£48,300) and that the Earl of Argyll should guarantee the money. Mackintosh was with great difficulty persuaded to sign an agreement to sell. The Earl of Argyll paid the money in 1666, and it was arranged that Lochiel should hold the lands under him. Mackintosh was enabled to pay off considerable burdens on his estates with the money from this sale. In effect Lochiel held the lands direct from the Crown, and still does to this day.

Thus ended the great feud which had lasted for three and a half centuries between the Clan Chattan and Clan Cameron, and the Highlands were no more troubled by their strife, indeed the two clans became great friends.

In 1667 came the beginning of the end of the feud with the Macdonalds of Keppoch concerning the lands occupied by the Macdonalds in Glenroy and Glenspean. These lands had been granted to Mackintosh by the King in the fifteenth century and the Macdonalds were his tenants, but they had seldom paid any rent and, in fact, they frequently aided his enemies. In 1572 Ronald of Keppoch gave a strict bond of allegiance to Lachlan Mor, the sixteenth Chief, but it was broken by his son who supported Huntly against Mackintosh in 1591. The Macdonalds raided Glenesk in 1667 and stole cattle from Lindsay of Edzell, who was Lachlan Mackintosh's father-in-law. This aroused Mackintosh's wrath, and he set out for Lochaber to hold his courts as hereditary Steward and to try the Macdonalds for this and other offences. He held four courts, one at Keppoch and three on Huntly's lands, and forced the Macdonalds to restore what they had taken.

In 1673 Mackintosh induced the Privy Council to order the Macdonalds to remove from Glenroy and Glenspean. On their disobeying the order they were declared rebels. As they still had not paid their rent, Mackintosh went to Keppoch with three hundred men, where he was met by Archibald Macdonald and his son Coll with promises to pay their dues. Archibald and Coll went with Mackintosh to Dunachton, where new leases were given to them and their clan.

The Macdonalds did not pay their arrears, and Mackintosh obtained a commission of fire and sword against them in 1681. Archibald had died, and his son, known as "Coll of the Cows," who now led the Macdonalds, was an adept at guerilla warfare. He made frequent raids, as his father had done before him, and his men would sweep down the Great Glen and spread consternation through Inverness. Coll offered submission to a legal decision, but Mackintosh "by a clandestine warrant" caused Coll to be taken and imprisoned in the Tolbooth at Inverness without a trial. This action by Mackintosh was censured as an ungenerous act, but he had to take a strong line as he held a magisterial position at Inverness as well as the Privy Council's commission. Coll was released on the authority of Mackintosh of Kinrara, the Chief's uncle. Huntly also protested against Coll's treatment and complained "that all Brae Lochaber is out-lawed by Mackintosh's malice."

In 1688 the Privy Council renewed the commission to Mackintosh against the Macdonalds, who owed twenty-five years' rent, and had defied the law of the land. The Council ordered the men of Inverness and the neighbouring shires to support Mackintosh and sent him a company of regular soldiers under Mackenzie of Suddie. The Macphersons did not follow the Chief, probably because of Huntly's influence, but they were in sympathy, as will be seen. Macdonald was followed by his clan, reinforced from Glengarry and Glencoe, and also by some of the Camerons.

The two forces met at Mulroy, where the Macdonalds had the advantage of a position on the crest of a hill. Mackintosh decided to attack them at once. The battle is described by a soldier called Donald McBean, as follows :

"Both parties (Mackintosh's and Suddies) were ordered to march up the hill. A company being in front we drew up in line of battle as we could, our Company (Suddies) being on the right. We were no sooner in order but there appears double our number of Macdonalds, which made us then fear the worst. At least for my part I repeated my former wish that I had been spinning tobacco in Inverness. The Macdonalds came down the hill upon us without either shoes or stockings or bonnets on their heads; they gave a shout and then the fight began on both sides and continued in hot dispute for an hour. Then they broke in upon us with sword and target and Lochaber axes, which obliged us to give way. Seeing my captain sore wounded and a great many more lying with their heads cloven on every side, I was sadly affrighted, never having seen the like before. A highland man attacked me with sword and targe and cut my wooden handled bayonet out of the muzzle of my gun. I then clubbed my gun and gave him a stroke with it which made the butt end fly off. Seeing the Highland men to come fast upon me, I took to my heels and ran thirty miles before I looked behind me. Every person I saw or met I took him for my enemy."

The Macdonalds, having superior numbers and the advantage of position, gained a decided victory, inflicting severe loss on the Mackintosh forces, and taking the Chief prisoner. The Macphersons arrived after the battle, and though they had refused to follow the Chief, they now bravely rescued him from the Macdonalds. However, the defeat was a great humiliation for the Mackintoshes. The battle of Mulroy, fought in 1688, is of considerable interest as being the last clan battle fought between Highlanders.

The Privy Council sent regular troops to punish the Macdonalds. This was done with great severity, and the troops burned the houses and crops of the clan, but most of the Macdonalds escaped to the hills, and Coll was not subdued.

In spite of this harsh treatment Keppoch rose in defence of James VII against William of Orange, Coll being sent by the western chiefs with eight hundred men to escort Viscount Dundee into Lochaber. Coll laid siege to Inverness, and here Dundee found him in 1689 with some of the leading citizens in his custody. Dundee wished to have the townspeople on his side and gave Coll a bond for two thousand dollars to make peace with them. Dundee then attempted to reconcile Keppoch and Mackintosh, but it was much too soon after the battle of Mulroy for Mackintosh to agree. Dundee then encouraged Keppoch to punish Mackintosh by driving off his cattle, after which Mackintosh would not assist Dundee in any way, although Mackintosh was well affected to the King.

Dundee's army went to Badenoch and Coll betook himself to Dunachton, where he burned Mackintosh's fine house, which had only been built fifteen years before (1675).

At the battle of Killiecrankie in 1689, only a few Mackintoshes took part. The Chief was not there because of Dundee's alliance with Keppoch. Dundee won a victory, but was killed, his opponent, Mackay, living to win the war for William and Mary.

Dundee's friends in no wise blamed Mackintosh for not joining the Jacobite army, and it is a fact that one of Dundee's relatives presented Mackintosh with the sword which Dundee wore at Killiecrankie. It is still preserved at Moy Hall, in company with the sword presented by Charles, Prince of Wales, in 1622 to Sir Lachlan, and these two swords are laid crossed on the coffin of every Chief of Mackintosh at his funeral.

In 1690 Mackintosh petitioned the Scots Parliament against Macdonald of Keppoch for burning Dunachton and harrying his lands in Badenoch, Strathdearn and Strathnairn. The Parliament issued two Acts in favour of Mackintosh, stating that he had sustained damage by the Macdonalds in Dunachton, Kinrara, Pittowrie, Kincraig, Dalnavert, Moy, Schiphin, and Lairgs and that tenants had been beggared and forced to flee from their homes.

Parliament recognised Mackintosh's right to the lands of Keppoch, Glenroy and Glenspean, but they gave him no practical assistance beyond these Acts. Mackintosh made another attempt in 1697 to dislodge the Macdonalds and put them to the horn (outlawed). This time King William III wrote to the Council, saying that their Lordships must find methods to enforce the law and to reduce the rebels, and to repossess Mackintosh as legal owner. In 1698 the Council renewed Mackintosh's commission of fire and sword against the Macdonalds, and all men between sixty and sixteen years old in Inverness, Ross, Nairn, Perth and Aberdeen were ordered to assist Mackintosh. Fort William, which was only twelve miles from Coll's house, was manned with a royal garrison. When Coll saw the vigorous measures taken against him by the King and Council, he entered into negotiation with Mackintosh, and the Macdonalds were not exterminated nor even removed from Keppoch, Coll signing a submission to the laird of Mackintosh and binding his followers to observe the same. Coll himself had to leave Keppoch until after the death of Lachlan Mackintosh. The feud was thus ended and the Macdonalds lived in peace as tenants of the Chiefs of Mackintosh for nearly a century.

Lachlan Mackintosh had acquired a wadset of the Castle and barony of Dalcross in 1688. After the destruction of Dunachton he intended living at Dalcross, instead of the castle in Loch Moy, which he found inconvenient. However, he found Dalcross equally inconvenient, so he built a new house at the north end of Loch Moy about 1700. The Chief, now a confirmed invalid, made over his estates to his son Lachlan in 1702. That same year the young Lachlan bought Dalcross Castle outright.

The Chief died at Dalcross in 1704 and was buried at Petty. His body lay in state for a month at Dalcross, during which time funeral feasts were kept up at great expense and the cooks and confectioners were brought from Edinburgh. Two thousand armed men attended the funeral and all the neighbouring chiefs with their followers, the procession extending for four miles. The extravagance of the arrangements embarrassed the family finances for many years afterwards.

CHAPTER VIII

LACHLAN, the twentieth Chief, succeeded his father in 1704, and the first ten years of his chiefship went by peacefully. At the time of Queen Anne's death, in 1714, the Earl of Mar was Secretary of State for Scotland. He drew up an address of loyalty to the new King, George I, and obtained the signatures of numerous Highland chiefs, including Mackintosh, Glengarry, Lochiel and Cluny. Mar hoped, by being the bearer of this address, to obtain power, irrespective of party, and to retain his influence in the new order of things. To his amazement and mortification George I refused to accept the address, or the services of the Earl, whereupon Lord Mar threw himself into the Jacobite cause, and called on the clans to assist him. A considerable force followed Mar, and he proclaimed James VIII King at Braemar. James, known as the Chevalier St. Georges, had been living in France at Bar-le-Duc, where one of the best-known soldiers of the Mackintosh clan, William the younger of Borlum, had been with him. William, who is described as " a gentleman of polite education and good knowledge," had been employed as a Jacobite agent for some years, and his wife, Mary Reade, had been maid of honour to the Princess Anne before she became Queen of England.

In 1714 Borlum returned to Scotland and was active in rallying supporters of the Stuarts. The Chief of Mackintosh placed Borlum in command of his forces and accompanied him to Inverness, where they proclaimed James VIII as King and seized such arms and public moneys as they could find. Hearing that there were some arms and ammunition at Culloden House, the Mackintoshes demanded possession of them. Mrs. Forbes, in the absence of her husband, doughtily refused, put her house in a state of defence and sent to Munro of Foulis for help. Munro was coming to her assistance when he was stopped by Seaforth, who was on the Jacobite side. However, Seaforth persuaded Mackintosh not to waste precious time storming a single house against a woman, but to march his eight hundred men south to join the Earl of Mar at Perth. There Mackintosh was given command of his own regiment, with the title of Colonel, and Borlum was given command of the whole brigade, with the title of Brigadier. It speaks well for the generosity of the Chief that he was willing to serve under his own clansman. He had thirty-two officers in the battalion, twenty-eight of whom bore Clan Chattan names. The Farquharsons of Invercauld joined with the Mackintoshes.

Lord Mar was no great soldier, and remained at Perth with the main body of troops. A better course would have been to move the force to Stirling to attack the Duke of Argyll, who occupied Stirling for the Government. Then the undecided clans would have probably rallied to the Jacobite standard.

Mar did not attack Stirling, but ordered Borlum to make a dash for Edinburgh, which entailed crossing the Forth. Mar sent some troops to make a feint at Burntisland, which drew off the English ships, but cost the capture of a thousand men. Borlum, with fifteen hundred men, including the Mackintosh regiment, succeeded in crossing from Pittenweem and Crail in open boats.

The Brigadier promptly marched on Edinburgh, where he hoped to be assisted by the Jacobites within the city. The city magistrates, however, upon hearing of Borlum's approach, had promptly lodged all the leading Jacobites in prison.

Borlum was too experienced a soldier to waste his little army by attempting to carry a big city by assault without any assistance from within, so he seized Leith instead and fortified himself in one of the forts built there by Cromwell. There he was attacked the following day by Argyll who, failing in his assault, was compelled to withdraw. Borlum, in obedience to orders received from Mar, thereupon marched his force south to join Lord Kenmure and the English Jacobites under Mr. Foster. He found them at Kelso, the Highlanders marching into the town playing their pipes. They seem to have inspired the natives with profound terror, and quite a hundred years later the name of Borlum was used as a bogey to frighten children. It must have been merely their wild appearance that produced this effect, for Borlum maintained good discipline.

Lord Kenmure took over supreme command of the army, and Borlum retained command of the Highland division. He advised Kenmure to attack the English under General Carpenter, who was known to be training recruits into cavalry. Kenmure rejected the advice and was to rue his decision at the fatal fight of Preston in 1715.

Borlum was also anxious to join the western clans under General Gordon and so to secure Scotland, rather than to penetrate England, where so far there had been no sign of a rising. His advice was again flouted, as M . Foster and Lord Widdrington assured Lord Kenmure that al Lancashire, being a nest of Catholics, would rise if the Scots marched in. Kenmure decided to advance into England and march into Lancashire. When the Scots then refused to cross the Border, in loyalty to his General, Borlum personally persuaded about a thousand Highlanders to follow, but five hundred others turned back and went home, though Borlum stood in the Esk swearing at them and calling them " reskels of humanity."

The fatal march began, but at Kendal and Appleby no recruits joined, and though Foster took over command from Kenmure he could not prevent a number of desertions. Foster entered Preston, raised the Jacobite standard and proclaimed King James, but although some of the neighbouring gentry joined him with their followers, they were sadly raw and untrained as troops. Foster planned an advance on Manchester, but was forced to give battle to defend Preston against General Wills with the Government forces. The Chief of Mackintosh commanded one defence force, Borlum another, Lord Charles Murray a third and Mr. Douglas a fourth. Things were not going so badly with the Jacobites at first, until Wills was reinforced by General Carpenter, whom Kenmure had neglected to destroy. This was too much for Foster, who gave up all hope and, without the knowledge of the Scots, sent a secret envoy to Wills to ask for terms. Wills ordered their surrender as rebels and demanded two leaders as hostages—one Scottish and one English. Accordingly the Chief of Mackintosh and the Earl of Derwentwater were placed in Wills' hands.

The Highlanders, on finding the surrender arranged, " were terribly enraged, and declared they would die fighting." They killed a good many who dared to talk to them of surrender. However, their fury was unavailing, and on Wills threatening with his superior force to kill every man of them the inevitable surrender took place.

General Wills took possession of Preston with fifteen hundred prisoners—of the rank and file were sixty bearing Clan Chattan names, including thirteen Mackintoshes and sixteen Macgillivrays.

The Chief and Borlum and others of note were sent to

London, but many of inferior rank were executed, and others transported to America for slavery, while some were imprisoned in various English towns.

The officers sent as prisoners to London were escorted from Highgate in a mock triumphal procession followed by a jeering mob. Mackintosh is described as "a brave and handsome gentleman," and Borlum as "remarkable for the grim ferocity of his scarred face." For five months they lay in prison, until in April 1716 their trial was to be held. On the night before this trial Borlum and fifteen others overpowered the sentinels and made their escape from prison; seven were recaptured, but the others, including Borlum, got safely away. Foster escaped in a separate venture. The Government issued a description of the Brigadier as "a Tall Rawboned Man about sixty years old, Fair-Complexioned, Beetle-Browed, Grey-Eyed, speaks Broad Scotch." They offered one thousand pounds reward for Borlum's capture, but he evaded pursuit and was assisted by his brother-in-law, Thomas Reade, in Oxfordshire, to conceal himself until he was able to find a ship to carry him to France.

The London mob, with whom Borlum was decidedly popular, was highly pleased with his escape. They celebrated his heroism in ballads not flattering to their own countrymen. The following ballad is quoted from Hogg's *Jacobite Relics of Scotland*:

Mackintosh was a soldier brave
And did most gallantly behave
When into Northumberland he came
With gallant men of his own name.
Then Derwentwater he did say
That five hundred guineas he would lay,
To beat the militia man to man;
But they proved cowards and off they ran.

Then the Earl of Mar did vow and swear
That English ground if he came near,
Ere the right should starve, and the wrong should stand,
He'd blow them all to some foreign land.
Lord Derwentwater he rode away,
Well mounted on his dapple gray;
But soon he wish'd him home with speed,
Fearing they were all betrayed indeed.

" Adzounds ! " cried Foster, " never fear.
" For Brunswick's army is not near ;
" And if they dare come, our valour we'll show,
" And give them a total overthrow."
But Derwentwater soon he found
That they were all enclosed around.
" Alack ! " he cried, " for this cowardly strife,
" How many brave men shall lose their life ! "

Old Mackintosh he shook his head,
When he saw his Highland lads lie dead ;
And he wept not for the loss of those,
But for the success of their proud foes.
Then Mackintosh unto Wills he came,
Saying, " I have been a soldier in my time,
" And ere a Scot of mine shall yield,
" We'll all lie dead upon the field."

" Then go your ways," he made reply ;
" Either surrender, or you shall die.
" Go back to your own men in the town :
" What can you do when left alone ? "
Mackintosh is a gallant soldier,
With his musket over his shoulder.
" Every true man point his rapier ;
" But, damn you, Foster, you are a traitor ! "

Lord Derwentwater to Foster said,
" Thou hast ruined the cause, and all betrayed ;
" For thou didst vow to stand our friend,
" But hast proved traitor in the end.
" Thou brought us from our own country ;
" We left our homes, and came with thee ;
" But thou art a rogue and a traitor both,
" And hast broke thy honour and thy oath."

Lord Derwentwater to Litchfield did ride.
With armed men on every side ;
But still he swore by the point of his sword,
To drink a health to his rightful Lord.
Lord Derwentwater he was condemned,
And led unto his latter end ;
And though his lady did plead full sore,
They took his life, they could get no more.

Brave Derwentwater he is dead;
From his fair body they took the head;
But Mackintosh and his friends are fled,
And they'll set the hat on another head.
And whether they are gone beyond the Sea,
Or if they abide in this country,
Though our King would give ten thousand pound,
Old Mackintosh will scorn to be found.

Borlum remained in France until 1719, when he landed on the west coast of Scotland with a Jacobite expedition. The Brigadier was with a small force of Scots and Spaniards under the Marquis of Tullibardine and the Earls of Marischal and Seaforth. They were joined by a few more of the Mackenzies, but were too weak to make a stand against the Government forces, and after a skirmish in Glenshiel they were disbanded, and the leaders returned to the Continent. Borlum, however, remained in Scotland, and though for a few years he kept out of the way, he was eventually captured and remained a prisoner until he died in 1743 at the age of eighty-five. During his captivity he wrote and published two pamphlets—a treatise on agriculture, and a scheme for curbing depredation in the Highlands. This scheme is mentioned thirty years later by the Reverend Lachlan Shaw, as being executed with success.

The Chief of Mackintosh was released from prison in August 1716, at the intercession of his wife and Lord Lovat and other friends, who pleaded that Lachlan had been "trepanned into the rebellion by the craft of the Brigadier"!

The exiled James VIII attempted to reward the Chief by creating him a peer with the title of Lord Mackintosh, and sent him a patent of nobility from Avignon. However, the Chief never made any attempt to take up this empty title.

After his release in 1716 the Chief devoted himself to improving his estates and to settling disputes. He found himself challenged by Macpherson of Cluny, who renewed the question so often raised by his family, of claiming to be Chiefs of Clan Chattan. The Macphersons had been growing in strength and importance, and in the sixteenth century the Huntly family had used them as instruments to weaken and thwart the Chiefs of Mackintosh. This went on in the seventeenth century, and in 1672 the Lord Lyon King of Arms had given judgment in favour of Mackintosh being Chief of Clan Chattan. In the eighteenth century Duncan Macpherson of Cluny regarded himself as head of the Macphersons and Chief of Old Clan Chattan. At his death in 1722 his successor, Lachlan Macpherson, agreed to a proposal that the question should be finally settled.

A meeting of the Clan Chattan was held at Moy in 1724, which was attended by large numbers of Mackintoshes, Macphersons, Macgillivrays, Macbeans and all other families of the clan. Cluny bound himself and his successors to recognise Mackintosh as the undoubted Chief of Clan Chattan. This was signed by Mackintosh and Cluny and many of those present, and in exchange Mackintosh gave up to Cluny and his heirs forever the lands of Gallovy with Kinloch, Muckoull, Inverviddan and Ardverikie.

After some years the Macphersons of Cluny repudiated this agreement, and renounced all dependence on the family of Mackintosh, but kept the lands which the agreement had obtained for him. Cluny made a bond of friendship with Lochiel and Lord Lovat.

Lachlan Mackintosh's wife, who survived him for nineteen years, was Anne Duff of Drummuir. He is described as of "middle stature, ruddy complexion, straight and lively. Having had a liberal education, Lachlan was courteous and polite in his address, his easy and ready wit, his free and facetious conversation, rendered him a most agreeable companion, and his strict and untainted honour and integrity endeared him to all ranks. He was a most affectionate husband, firm friend, kind master and indulgent Chief, and though he had no children of his own, he acted as parent to the younger gentlemen of the clan, and particularly to his near relations."

Lachlan died at Moy in 1731, aged about sixty years. The funeral was delayed for two months owing to the absence of his successor, and the body lay in state at Dalcross. As with previous funerals of Mackintosh chiefs, the expenses were enormous, and burdened the estate for years. Several thousand persons attended the burial at Petty.

CHAPTER IX

WILLIAM, the twenty-first Chief, succeeded in 1731. He was a second cousin of the late Chief, and a great-grandson of Sir Lachlan, the seventeenth Chief. William had been in the Army, but he now set himself to relieving the estate of its burdens, and he cleared off some two thousand pounds in debts. For this reason, as the Reverend Lachlan Shaw says, " he did not effect the clannish grandeur, the numerous attendants and servants, common among Highland chieftains. He abridged the number of servants and cut off much of the superfluous expenses of his family." Shaw also says, " His life was a pattern of virtue and goodness." In those days it was the custom to fight duels, and William fought his share. At this time an officer named Graeme had possession of Dundee's sword, which Lachlan had given up to him after the battle of Preston. William challenged Graeme either to give up the sword, or fight a duel, but fortunately Captain Graeme agreed peacefully to return the famous sword, which is still preserved at Moy Hall.

William married Christian Menzies of Castle Menzies, but they had no children. Christian died before her husband, who was much upset by her death. William was a delicate man, who to improve his health went to the South of France, but returned to Edinburgh, where he died in 1740. He was buried at Holyrood, his funeral expenses were very moderate and none of the usual extravagance was allowed.

ANGUS, the twenty-second Chief, succeeded his brother in 1740. In his time was made the last great attempt to restore the Stuarts to the throne.

The English Government took drastic measures to overawe the Highland clans, and were much hated as a result. They built forts for English garrisons, and made new roads for the movements of troops. They gave orders to deprive all Highlanders of their arms. The clans in favour of the Government gave up their arms at once, being anxious to show their obedience, but the Jacobites, however, only gave up old and useless weapons and managed to conceal a great many which were serviceable. They also hindered the road-making wherever they could, and used to block the roads by night, and some parts of the road had to be re-laid many times over, thus compelling the troops under the command of General Wade to place pickets all the way, on guard.

The decision taken in 1743 to send abroad the Black Watch regiment, which had been raised for home service only and for preserving order in the Highlands, increased the resentment of the Highlands in general, and the Clan Chattan in particular. A protest was made against this order, and the men were told their destination was Edinburgh, for the purpose of being reviewed. Arriving at Edinburgh, they were moved to Berwick, and then to London, where they were told that the King would inspect them. They were reviewed by General Wade, as the King had gone to Hanover. The men developed a suspicion that they were to be transported to America, and many of them resolved to escape. They started off for Scotland, but only reached Northampton, where they were captured. They were taken back to London and tried as deserters. Three, all of Clan Chattan, were executed, their names being Samuel Macpherson, Malcolm Macpherson and Farquhar Shaw. The rest of the offenders were sent abroad to garrisons in the Mediterranean, the West Indies and America.

News of the discontent in Scotland was carried to France, where the so-called James VIII and his son, Prince Charles Edward, were living. The Prince declared his intention of overthrowing King George II and of placing his father on the throne. He set out for Scotland in a French ship, landing in the Western Highlands in July 1745. He had only seven followers with him, but Lochiel and many other Highlanders soon rallied, and Prince Charles raised his standard at Glenfinnan, on Loch Shiel, in August. From there the Prince marched to Edinburgh and proclaimed his father King with startling success. The Macphersons now joined him under Ewan, younger of Cluny. Charles won a victory at Prestonpans and defeated General Cope with the Government army.

Prince Charles wasted some weeks holding court in Edinburgh, and then set out on his ill-fated march to London. However, at Derby it was decided in a Council of War to return to Scotland, and the army sadly retraced its steps. A party of Clan Chattan supporters joined the Prince at Stirling on his return. Cluny Macpherson attempted to enlist other Mackintoshes in Badenoch. However, the Chief of Mackintosh did not join the Prince, but continued to hold his commission under King George II and to command a company of the Black Watch. The Chief's wife, Anne Farquharson of Invercauld, though only twenty years old, took up the Prince's cause, and raised the clan without any hindrance from her husband. In his absence she inspected the clan regiment before it left for Stirling, selecting MacGillivray of Dunmaglas as Colonel.

Under MacGillivray the Clan Chattan regiment of eight hundred strong fought in the battle of Falkirk. They and the Macphersons fought side by side in the centre of the front line, with the Farquharsons of Balmoral next on the right. The Prince's army won the victory at Falkirk in 1746, but though Charles wanted to follow up his advantage, the Chiefs advised him to retreat in order to take the northern forts, and then to recruit a larger army.

Accordingly, the Jacobite force moved back to the north, but the forts were not taken nor the roads destroyed. The Prince arrived at Moy on 16th February 1746 with only a few attendants, where he was received by the Lady Mackintosh. The Camerons, with five hundred men, encamped at Moybeg; the Government troops of seventeen hundred strong, under Lord Loudon, were at Inverness. The Lady Mackintosh sent out Donald Fraser, the Smith at Moy, with four other men to watch the road from Inverness. About midnight, when they became aware of the approach of a body of troops, Fraser posted his men among a number of peat-stacks which might be mistaken in the darkness for groups of men. When Loudon's troops came near Fraser and his men fired their guns and ran in various directions shouting loudly for Mackintoshes, Camerons and Macdonalds to advance. The ruse was successful, and the army fell back in alarm to Inverness. At the same time a small boy was smuggled out of Inverness by old Lady Mackintosh, who was Anne Duff, widow of the twentieth Chief, to warn the Prince of Loudon's approach. The boy was secretly carried out on horseback under the cloak of a dragoon, and once outside the town he slipped off the horse to make his way by short-cuts to Moy. He gave the alarm, the Prince was aroused and left Moy Hall to join Lochiel's men, who were preparing to make a stand, when a messenger came to tell them of the Smith's success, which came to be known as the Rout of Moy. The Smith's sword and anvil are still kept at Moy Hall, and so are Prince Charles' bonnet and the bed he slept in.

Lord Loudon, thinking the Jacobite army much larger than it actually was, withdrew his troops immediately from Inverness. Accordingly, Prince Charles took possession of the town as his headquarters, staying for two months in the house of the dowager Anne Lady Mackintosh, in Church Street.

Charles now found his forces greatly augmented. He sent one detachment to take Fort Augustus, and another, under the Duke of Perth, into Ross-shire to pursue Lord Loudon. The Duke had with him the Mackenzie, Mackintosh and Mackinnon regiments, also some Macgregors and Macdonalds. Loudon's force was dispersed, and a large number of prisoners captured, among whom was the Chief of Mackintosh. The Prince sent Mackintosh to his own wife at Moy, saying that he could not be in better security or more honourably treated.

On 14th April 1746, news reached Inverness that the Duke of Cumberland's army had crossed the Spey, and the Prince moved to Culloden, from which place he advanced with his first troop of Life Guards and the Mackintosh regiment as far as the Loch of the Clans, within four miles of Nairn. His army bivouacked that night in the woods of Culloden, he himself and his principal officers occupying Culloden House. On the following day the army was drawn up on Culloden moor in expectation of the enemy's advance, but no enemy appeared. This was in some respects satisfactory, as the Jacobites were much under strength, and the delay would enable many absentees (among whom were the Macphersons, Frasers, Mackenzies and other clans) to come up. It seems inexplicable how the Prince, being in a friendly country, should not have heard of Cumberland's approach until the Duke was within a day's march of him. The absence of so large a part of his force from headquarters at such a critical moment can be explained by the bad commissariat arrangements which made it difficult to feed those who remained with Charles. The clans assembled with great rapidity when called up, and Charles was assured that they would all be forthcoming when required, and that until then it was better to allow them to live and feed in their own homes. Thus the Macphersons had been left in Badenoch and were actually on their way to the battle when they were met by their fugitive friends after it was over.

The Jacobite leaders, thinking that the Duke of Cumberland would celebrate his birthday, decided on a night attack while the Duke's men would be sleeping off the effects of their festivity. The Jacobites had about ten miles to travel, and as they started at eight o'clock in the evening they should have been there by midnight. However, they had not come up with the enemy by two o'clock in the morning, and all hope of a surprise attack was abandoned. The weary and half-famished Highlanders were led back to the fatal moor of Culloden, which they reached about five o'clock in the morning. News came that the enemy was advancing, and the Jacobite army was at once drawn up in battle array. They were nearly starving, and the only food they obtained was one biscuit per man. Some others had gone into Inverness to find food for themselves. The enemy consisted of eight thousand fresh, well-fed troops, supported by plenty of cavalry and cannon.

The battle began at one p.m. on 16th April. The Camerons were placed on the right, with the Mackintoshes in the centre and the Macdonalds on the left. Charles had unfortunately selected for their battlefield the open moor where Cumberland's horse could make good use of the ground. Another blunder was that Charles kept his little force waiting to be attacked. For some time they stood firm and were raked by a terrible cannon fire, while to add to their misery a snowstorm beat mercilessly on their faces. The Mackintosh regiment, unable longer to refrain, broke from the front line and charged, to be followed by the rest of the first line. The Macdonalds, sulking about being deprived of the right wing, did not attack and allowed themselves to be mown down by the cannon. Had they attacked, the issue might have been different.

What followed was a foregone conclusion. The Highlanders rushed ahead in a last despairing charge; regardless of their hunger, regardless of their frozen limbs, driven to frenzy by their misery and inspired by hatred of their English foes, the little band swept forward to its doom. Not once did it falter though three lines of steady muskets, and cannon loaded with grape-shot made cruel gaps in its ranks. Forward it rushed. It reached its goal, broke through the first line of the English, whom it swept aside like chaff; almost reached the second line, and then it melted, literally mown down. All that loyalty, all that heroism could do was done that day, and done in vain.

Unsupported by the rest of the army the first forlorn hope could do no more. The Mackintosh regiment which led the fatal charge suffered the most severely, and more Mackintoshes were killed than any other clan. Out of seventeen officers only three were surviving. The day after the battle the Highlanders were found lying in heaps three or four deep, so eager were those behind to reach their foes. To-day the tragic field of Culloden is marked with grave-stones inscribed with the names of the clans who fell there, and so numerous were the Mackintosh casualties that their massed graves are commemorated by three grave-stones.

John Roy's poem, " The Day of Culloden," says :

" Redoubled are shed my tears for the dead,
As I think of Clan Chattan the foremost in fight ;
O woe for the time that has shrivelled their prime,
And woe that the left had not stood at the right."

The rush took place so suddenly and lasted so few minutes that Charles had not time to support it by moving forward his second line. In vain he sought to rally the fugitives and to move forward, but the second line had seen the fate of its comrades of the first line and was thrown into confusion by the survivors retreating upon it. And now the Campbells had pulled down a wall which protected the Jacobites' flank, so that Cumberland's dragoons came charging down upon them, ending the fight. The miserable remnant of as brave a band as ever stood to arms—" their hearts broken with despair rather than terror "—gave way and the dragoons mercilessly hacked them to pieces.

The whole battle, which had lasted about forty minutes, now became a terrible slaughter. As for the unhappy Prince, unwilling to believe that all was lost and ready to sacrifice his own life, he lingered until his friends forced him from the fatal field. From then onwards he was a hunted fugitive, until he managed to escape safely into France, but his campaign had been entirely defeated, and the hopes of the Stuart cause extinguished.

Cumberland pursued his victorious march to Inverness, which he entered without opposition. There he stayed in the house of the Dowager Lady Mackintosh, in the very room and the same bed which Prince Charles had so lately occupied. The old lady, in speaking afterwards of those events, was wont to remark :

"I've had two King's bairns living with me in my time, and to tell you the truth I wish I may never have another." She was confined for fourteen days in the common guard, as were also several other ladies attached to the Jacobite cause. The whole of the "disaffected country" was placed under severe martial law, cattle were driven off, and innocent men and women were shot without pity. Parties were sent out to ravage the country, and one of these parties made its way two days after Culloden battle to Moy, where they drove off the cattle and behaved with the utmost roughness to the Lady Mackintosh herself.

The Minister of the parish, hoping to curb the lawlessness of the soldiers by his presence, hastened to Moy Hall, but the worthy man found that the soldiers regarded him not at all, and that he might as well have remained at home. One asked him the time, and when he drew forth his watch, it was snatched from him. The Lady Mackintosh offered the snatcher money if he would restore it. "Oh, you have money," he cried, and her purse of fifty guineas, all she possessed, was rudely taken from her. When pressed by others to give them money, she replied truly that she had none, whereupon one ruffian struck her, but one of his comrades dragged him off, threatening him with dire penalties "if he touched that lady." Lady Mackintosh recognised in her champion a soldier whom she had once begged off from a flogging. Fortunately for her, a party of dragoons now arrived at Moy under Sir Everard Fawkner, the Duke's secretary, and an old admirer of Anne's. On seeing her, he exclaimed, "Can this be Anne Farquharson!" and flinging himself from his horse hastened to greet her. He protected her from any further rudeness, though it was his duty to arrest her and convey her to Inverness by the Duke's order. He mounted her on the only horse left at Moy, and escorted her most civilly to Inverness, where she was imprisoned in her own room for six weeks, but was so far well treated that she was able to supply some of the poorer Jacobites with bread.

Two years later, Lady Mackintosh visited London, where she was a great favourite and much fêted. She attended a ball given by the Duke of Cumberland, and the first tune played was "Up and waur them a', Willie," to which the Duke asked her to dance with him. She did so, and then asked her partner whether, as she had danced to his tune, he would dance to hers. As a great gallant he could not refuse, and the Lady Mackintosh asked for "The Auld Stuarts back again," to which they accordingly danced together.

In consequence of a Government order to deprive the Jacobites of their arms, a party was sent to Strathdearn to seize all weapons. Grant of Dalrachny went to Moy and took the famous swords, which were heirlooms, to wit, the swords of Charles I and of Dundee, and two dating from the battle of the North Inch, 1396. Mackintosh at once got Lord Loudon to ask the Duke to have them restored. This was granted, but Mackintosh got word that his family papers were being destroyed. He hastened to Moy, where he found that the Grants had seized many Charters and documents which had been placed for safety in the Castle on the island. The Grants were already burning the precious papers, but Mackintosh had a force of two hundred men and dispersed the evil-doers and saved most of his valuable records.

The battle of Culloden marked the end of the clan system in Scotland as a military force. The Government abolished the hereditary jurisdiction of the chiefs, freed the tenants from giving service in exchange for their lands, forbade, under severe penalties, the carrying of arms and prohibited the wearing of Highland dress or tartan. The titles of the chiefs survived, and a strong feeling of loyalty in the individual clans still exists to-day, but the Jacobite rebellion expired in a wave of glory.

CHAPTER X

ÆNEAS, the twenty-third Chief, succeeded on the death of his uncle, Angus, in 1770. During the American War of Independence Æneas raised a company for the Second Battalion of Fraser's Highlanders, under Simon Fraser, son of Lord Lovat. He went to America in 1776 and fought in the battle of Brooklyn, and in the campaigns from 1777 to 1781. When Lord Cornwallis capitulated, Æneas and his men were taken prisoners, and were held until the war ended. He returned home in 1783 and devoted himself to his estates, where he did considerable planting of trees, and wrote an account of the family and the neighbourhood.

In Æneas's time Moy Hall was accidentally burned down, and in about 1800 he built a new residence, the present Moy Hall, at the north end of Loch Moy. Æneas entailed the estates first to heirs-male and then heirs-female of his own body, and failing them to a long list of consecutive heirs which included both males and females, and naming first his second cousin Alexander.

At this time a legend arose that the Mackintosh family was cursed, because three Mackintosh chiefs had died without a son to succeeded them. A poem called "The Curse of Moy," by Morrit of Rokeby, appeared in 1802 in Scott's *Minstrelsy of the Scottish Borders*. The story went that a chief of Mackintosh had been rejected as a suitor by Margaret, daughter of Grant of Glenmoriston. She accepted Grant of Alva, but Mackintosh captured him and the lady and her father, and imprisoned them all in his castle. Mackintosh asked Margaret to choose whether her father or her lover should be put to death, and when she asked for her lover to be spared Mackintosh was so enraged that he had both the men killed. Margaret became insane and wandered among the mountains of Badenoch, calling down a curse on the murderer's family:

> "That never the son of a Chief of Moy
> Might live to protect his father's age,
> Or close in peace his dying eye,
> Or gather his gloomy heritage."

This story was without foundation on fact, but was widely believed, the more so that Æneas was childless, and also the next chief after him, who was the fifth to have no son to succeed him.

King George III created Æneas a baronet in 1812, but as he left no issue the title died with him in 1820.

ALEXANDER, the twenty-fourth Chief, a merchant in Jamaica, succeeded his third cousin in 1820. He built Daviot House, on the left bank of the River Nairn, and lived there because the widow of the late Chief had the liferent of Moy Hall. He died unmarried in 1827.

ANGUS, the twenty-fifth Chief, succeeded his brother in 1827. He had settled in Canada, at a place which he called Moy. He owned numerous ships on the big lakes, and became a member of the Legislative Council of Canada. During the war of the Niagara Frontier with the United States in 1813, he afforded the Government valuable assistance at considerable loss to himself. He married Archange St. Martin, daughter of an officer in the French army under Montcalm. He returned to Scotland on the death of his brother, and assumed his position as Chief until he died in 1833. It is advisable here to give details of his family. He had four sons—Duncan, Alexander, Æneas and James St. Martin, and several daughters. Duncan, the eldest son, died unmarried in 1824. Alexander, the twenty-sixth Chief, had no children by his first wife, so his next brother, Æneas, regarded as the heir, was given Daviot in order that he might gain experience in looking after the estates. Æneas was married twice and had three sons and three daughters—Æneas, who was accidentally shot as a young man; Alexander, who was the father of Duncan Alexander; Duncan Houston, who had three sons, Lachlan, Malcolm and Duncan; Mary, who became Mrs. Granville Kekewich; Charlotte, who married William Stirling of Fairburn; Ada, who married Robert Graham Campbell of Shirvan.

The fourth son of the twenty-fifth Chief, James St. Martin, lived in Canada. His son, Alexander, settled in Honolulu and became the Reverend Canon Alexander Mackintosh, and had two sons, Æneas and Arthur. Æneas returned to England and became the Reverend Canon Mackintosh in Oldham, and has a son, Æneas, who served in the Royal Air Force during the Second World War. Arthur remained in Honolulu and became an American citizen. He has a son, Alexander, who served in the United States Army Air Force and was at the airfield at Pearl Harbour in 1941 during the Japanese attack.

Duncan Houston was in the Hong Kong and Shanghai Bank. He married Louisa Kekewich, daughter of the Right Honourable Mr. Justice Sir Arthur Kekewich, P.C., and had three sons and two daughters: Lachlan Donald, the eldest, entered the Royal Navy, and his career is described later in this book. Malcolm, the second son saw active service with the Cameron Highlanders in the First World War. Duncan, the third son, joined the Shell Oil Company, and is now the General Manager in Cairo. He was awarded the O.B.E. in 1946. Evelyn, the elder daughter served in the First World War as an officer in the Women's Royal Naval Service; she caught influenza on duty and died in 1918. Moulie, the younger daughter, was killed in an air raid in London in 1941.

CHAPTER XI

ALEXANDER, the twenty-sixth Chief, succeeded his father in 1833, and was the first son since 1704 to succeed a Chief of Mackintosh. He married firstly, Mary, daughter of John Glass, and after her death, Charlotte, daughter of Macleod of Dalvey, by whom he had six children. Alexander's daughter, Isabella, married Charles Part, and had six children.

Alexander died at Dunachton in 1861. He was described " as an excellent Landlord, a good countryman, estimable in family and social relations and a Mackintosh to the backbone."

ALEXANDER ÆNEAS, twenty-seventh Chief, succeeded his father in 1861. He was educated at Harrow and Cambridge. He afterwards raised and commanded a strong company of the Inverness-shire Volunteers, known as the Mackintosh Company, and later received a commission as Captain in the Royal Highland Light Infantry (Inverness-shire) Militia. After visiting North America and India, he settled down to the improvement of his estates, and enlarged and beautified Moy Hall. He married Frances, daughter of Sir Frederick Graham of Netherby in 1875. He died a few months later, and his widow had a posthumous daughter, Eva Hermione, who married Sir Godfrey Baring. Frances Mackintosh married the Earl of Verulam as her second husband.

ALFRED DONALD, the twenty-eighth Chief of Mackintosh and twenty-ninth of Clan Chattan, succeeded his brother in 1876. Born in 1851, he was educated at Cheltenham College and the Royal Military College, Sandhurst, joining the Highland Light Infantry in 1870. Soon after he became the Chief he left the Army and obtained a Militia company of the Highland Light Infantry. Later on, he joined the third battalion Cameron Highlanders, and succeeded to the command of the regiment in 1897, retiring in 1903. He took the keenest pride and personal interest in his clansmen, tenants and estates, also adding to Moy Hall. In 1914, although over sixty years old, he volunteered for service, and commanded his old regiment, the 3rd Cameron Highlanders, at Invergordon, until Lochiel resumed command in 1917. He became Lord Lieutenant of Inverness-shire in 1905, and was awarded the C.B.E. in 1919. He took a very prominent part in the administrative affairs of the country, having been Vice-Convener of the County Council since its establishment in 1890, and Convener for over twenty years.

Alfred was a keen sportsman, a first-class shot, and was Master of the Glamorgan Hounds. He was a personal friend of H.M. King George V, whom he entertained on several occasions at Moy Hall. Among the Royal visitors were also H.M. Queen Mary, the Duke and Duchess of York (now H.M. King George VI and H.M. Queen Elizabeth).

In 1921, when King George V was staying at Moy, a Cabinet Meeting was held at Inverness to discuss the Irish Treaty, and the Prime Minister, Mr. Lloyd George, was summoned to Moy.

The Chief sold Dunachton in 1937, this property having belonged to his family since 1497.

Alfred married Harriet Diana Arabella Mary, only child and heiress of Mr. Edward Priest Richard of Plas Newydd, Glamorganshire. She was a perfect hostess and " Lady Bountiful " at Moy. She was a keen rider to hounds and an expert fisher. She killed a 43-lb. salmon in the River Spean. She and her husband always lived half the year at Moy Hall and the other half at Cottrell, near Cardiff. During the First World War, Arabella Mackintosh ran her own Red Cross hospital at Inverness, for which she was awarded the C.B.E. She survived her husband by three years.

Alfred had an only son, Angus Alexander, born 1885. He entered the Army, and as a Captain in the Royal Horse Guards was badly wounded at Ypres in 1914, and was subsequently appointed Aide-de-Camp to the Governor-General of Canada. He married Lady Maud Cavendish, eldest daughter of the Duke of Devonshire, in 1917. For the last year of his life he was on the Military Staff of the British Ambassador in Washington. He died from pneumonia in 1918, leaving a daughter, Anne Peace Arabella, known as Arbell, who was born in that year.

It is here convenient to enumerate the estates during the chiefship of Alfred Donald, as they probably reached the peak of their fame. Alfred had developed them very highly and the Moy moors were renowned as amongst the best grouse moors in Scotland. The tables on opposite page show the acreage of the various estates, and the maximum number of grouse and stags killed in one year ; the date is shown in brackets.

Estate	Acres	Grouse (single birds)	Stags
Moy . . .	11,000	8,178 (1910)	—
Meallmore . .	9,475	5,400 (1935)	—
Daviot . . .	5,140	1,141 (1936)	—
Tordarroch . .	1,720	730 (1935)	—
Coignafearn . .	39,000	5,000 (1913)	86 (1938)
Glenspean . .	23,258	1,099 (1913)	—
Glenroy . . .	8,825	503 (1924)	—
Dunachton . .	10,774	4,830 (1932)	25 (1929)
Glenfeshie . .	5,500	91 (1922)	—
Dalcross . . .	1,058	—	—

Three specimen game totals killed at Moy are shown below.

Game	Year 1907	Year 1910	Year 1912
Grouse . . .	6,705	8,178	6,273
Blackgame . .	23	4	7
Partridges . .	11	26	7
Pheasants . .	1,909	1,317	740
Brown Hares . .	51	15	51
Blue Hares . .	3,012	1,672	2,673
Rabbits . . .	4,952	4,436	7,527
Woodcock . .	47	38	31
Wildfowl . .	4	217	7
Roe Deer . .	31	25	13
Snipe . . .	13	23	38
Various . .	44	53	19
TOTAL . .	16,802	16,004	17,436

In 1901 no less than nine hundred and fourteen brace of grouse were killed in one day at Moy.

The Chief died at Moy in 1938 and was buried at Petty. His character was of the greatest integrity and uprightness. He was a very prominent and distinguished figure in the Highlands, of a most courteous and generous nature and was beloved by all who knew him.

In his will he left all the Mackintosh estates and family heirlooms to his cousin Lachlan, who was the son of Duncan, whose father was third son of Æneas of Daviot, son of Angus the twenty-fifth Chief. It must be noted that in 1877 Alfred had ended the entail of Sir Æneas, twenty-third Chief. Now Alfred's will turned out to be an instance of the exercise by the Chief of the old power of nomination of a successor, which is called Tanistry. Lachlan then became the twenty-ninth Chief of Mackintosh as being the Inheritor of the " duthus " or principal estate of Moy and the family seals and banner, so the Lord Lyon King of Arms confirmed to him the arms of The Mackintosh of Mackintosh, and he thus entered into the historic inheritance of Moy, which has been for more than six centuries the seat of the Mackintosh chiefs and the heart of the race of Mackintosh.

In the settlement of Alfred there was no nomination of the Clan Chattan chiefship. Therefore at his death occurred the separation of the chiefships of Clan Chattan and Mackintosh. The heretrix of Clan Chattan was Arbell, the late Chief's grand-daughter; she was left the liferent of Dalcross Castle. She became the thirtieth Chief of Clan Chattan, but was Chief only until her marriage in 1942 with Major Anthony Warre, M.C., 12th Royal Lancers, thus abandoning the registered name of the Clan Chattan arms and chiefship. During the war she drove a car for the Red Cross in London in the most severe air raids from 1941. She lives at Dalcross, which she has now purchased, and has two sons—Angus and Jonathan.

In 1942 the chiefship of Clan Chattan thus devolved on Duncan Alexander, whose father was the second son of Æneas of Daviot. To him the Lord Lyon confirmed the arms of the Clan Chattan in 1947 in the name of Mackintosh of Mackintosh-Torcastle.

Duncan Alexander, thirty-first Chief of Clan Chattan, was born in 1883. He was educated at Bedford Modern School. He fought in the Boer War, and afterwards joined the Mounted Police. He married Ellen Primrose Smith in 1912. He owns a farm called Fairburn, near Felixburg, in South Rhodesia. He has two sons, Kenneth, born 1916, and Robert, born 1926. Kenneth served in the Army in North Africa in the Second World War. Kenneth married Margaret Farmer in 1945, and has a son called Duncan Alexander John, who was born in 1946.

Duncan Alexander's eldest brother, Æneas, accompanied Sir Ernest Shackleton on his Antarctic Expeditions in 1907 and 1914.

In the first expedition Æneas lost an eye, and in the second expedition he was placed in command of a sledging party in search of a missing team of explorers, in which search he died.

LACHLAN, twenty-ninth Chief of Mackintosh, was born in 1896. Educated at Cheam School, he entered the Navy in 1909, and went to the R.N. Colleges of Osborne and Dartmouth. He went to sea as a Cadet in 1913, serving throughout the First World War in the North Sea, mostly in destroyers, and was awarded the Distinguished Service Cross. He commanded the destroyer *Medea*, as a Lieutenant, in 1919.

After the war he specialised in naval aviation, qualifying in the first course of Naval Air Observers in 1921. He learned to fly in 1925. After serving in many aircraft carriers, he was promoted to Commander in 1930. He commanded the destroyers *Brazen* and *Boadicea*, and he was promoted to Captain in 1938.

In the Second World War Captain Mackintosh commanded the cruiser *Charybdis* and the aircraft carrier *Eagle*, from which he was saved, with most of his crew, when the *Eagle* was sunk while escorting a convoy to Malta in 1942. He was in the aircraft carrier *Victorious* as Chief of Staff to Sir Lumley Lyster, Rear-Admiral, Aircraft Carriers, when the North African landings took place in 1942, and was awarded the Distinguished Service Order for his services in the Mediterranean. He next commanded the *Victorious*, which formed part of the United States Fleet in the South Pacific in 1943. He was awarded the Legion of Merit with degree of Commander by the President of the United States for his services there. He was Chief of Staff to Vice-Admiral Sir Henry Moore, Second in Command of the Home Fleet for the successful naval air attack which disabled the German battleship *Tirpitz* in 1944. In 1944 he commissioned the new aircraft carrier *Implacable*, leaving her at the end of the year to become an Assistant Chief of the Naval Staff (Air) at the Admiralty, in the rank of Acting Rear-Admiral. He was made a Companion of the Order of the Bath for "distinguished services throughout the War in Europe." He was Flag Officer Flying Training from 1945 to 1947, and was appointed an Aide-de-Camp to H.M. The King for six months in 1947, and was promoted to Rear-Admiral in that year. In 1948 he was appointed to the Admiralty as Chief of Naval Air Equipment, and Chief Naval Representataive at the Ministry of Supply.

Lachlan married Margaret Elizabeth Darroch, daughter of

Lieutenant Colonel Darroch of Gourock and Torridon, in 1927. She worked with the Air Raid Precautions Services from 1939 to 1941 in the Portsmouth area, and later with the Women's Voluntary Services in Inverness-shire.

They have one son, Lachlan Ronald Duncan, born in 1928. He was educated at Elstree School, and entered the Navy in 1942 at the R.N. College, Dartmouth, to become a Sub-Lieutenant in 1947.

Lachlan found the estates embarrassed by death duties, and in a very unsound financial condition, further complicated by the Second World War. In order to pay off the serious burdens of debt the Trustees found it necessary to sell a large proportion of the estates. Brae Lochaber, including Glenspean and Glenroy, were the first to be sold, then Coignafearn, Daviot, Tordarroch, Glenfeshie and Meallmore. His cousin Arbell, the twenty-eighth Chief's granddaughter, had been left the liferent of Dalcross, which she purchased outright in 1944. Lachlan was able to retain Moy Hall and the Moy estate, also the Doune at Daviot.

The following paragraph is a description of Moy from the manuscript of Sir Æneas, twenty-third Chief:

> "Heaven has been very attentive to this place, for in advancing to and going from it on all sides the Country is rough and barren, which serves as a background, and sets off the whole to advantage; health resides in the peaceful vale, and the cool lympid stream gushes from every Rock, the heath covered Mountains feed the bleating sheep, and playful kid, which furnish healthy Meals to the Swains, the honest Ox, and lowing sweet breathing Cow give flesh and milk to the Sturdy Plowman, the Air and Water furnish wholesome food easily got at, cool shady Groves are not wanting to indulge meditation, and every object round us makes the grateful heart praise the Great Giver of Good for granting them."

Moy was considered a safe area for evacuee children in the Second World War, and some arrived in the village from Edinburgh in 1939, when several were housed in the estate factor's house. Then, in 1940, a German aircraft dropped a line of four bombs, aimed at Moy Hall, the nearest of which fell within two hundred yards of the house. The only damage they caused was some broken windows. Later on, some sixty little Clydeside boys and girls were received in Moy Hall for a few months, but it was too cold for them there in the winter.

Afterwards, in 1944, the house was used as a headquarters

for an armoured brigade for a short time before our successful invasion of Normandy.

It has been shown throughout their history that the Clan Chattan and the Mackintoshes are a stalwart, fearless and adventurous people. Three of their chiefs were murdered and two were imprisoned. Their patriotism and loyalty have carried them through in peace and war. The clan spirit is as strong as ever, and binds the clansmen together in all parts of the world. In the two World Wars many of the Clan Chattan men and women took their full share, and it is certain that should the country need them again the clan will respond as they have always done before.

Genealogical Table of the Chiefs of Mackintosh & Chiefs of Clan Chattan
showing also the principal branches of the Clan Mackintosh

Note: *The numbers in circles refer to* Chiefs of Mackintosh & *the numbers in squares to* Chiefs of Clan Chattan.

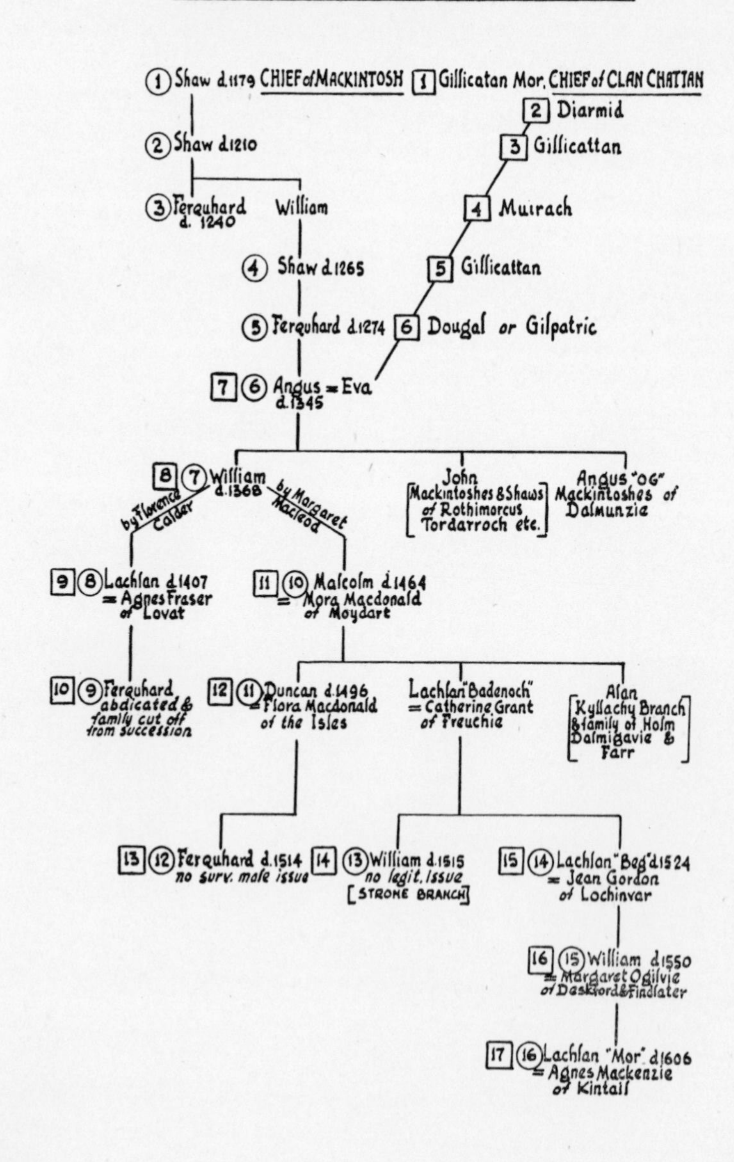

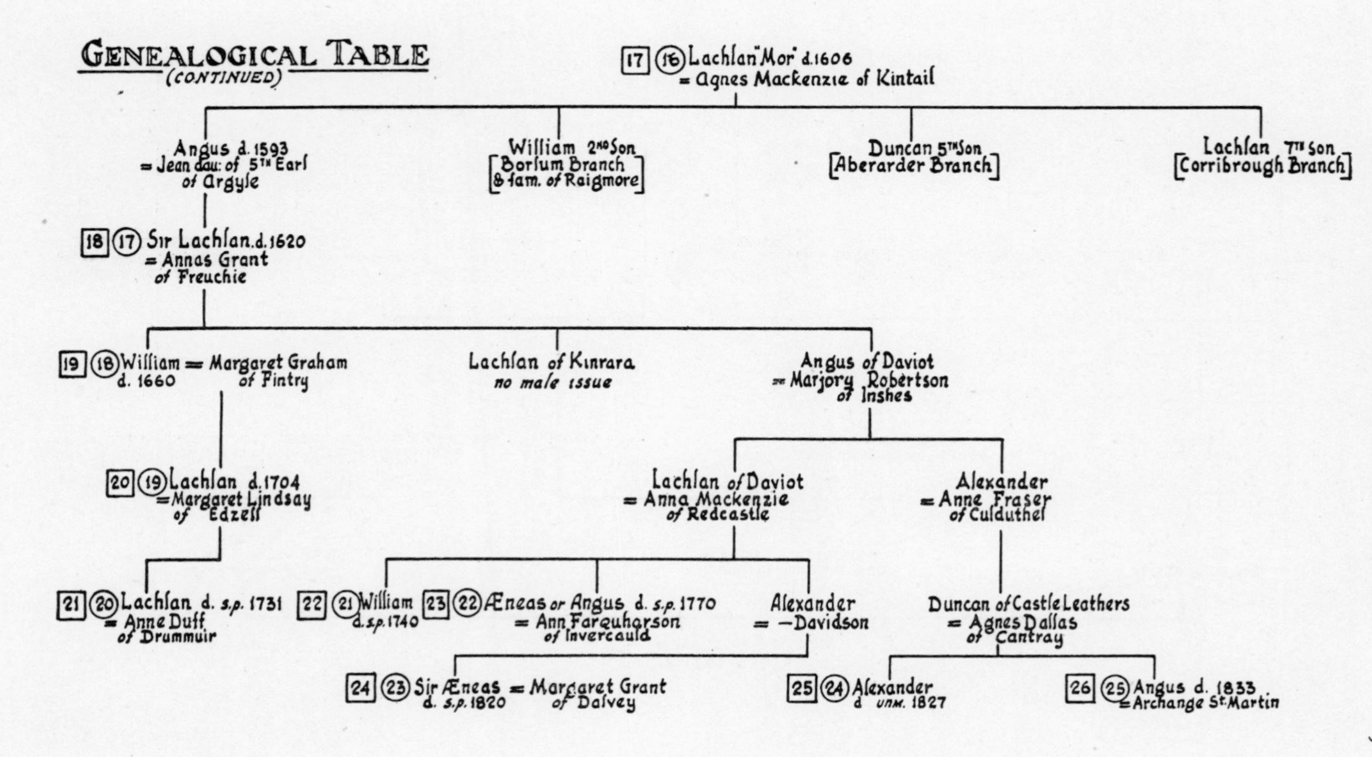
GENEALOGICAL TABLE
(CONTINUED)
17 16 Lachlan "Mor" d. 1606
= Agnes Mackenzie of Kintail
Angus d. 1593
= Jean dau: of 5th Earl of Argyle
William 2nd Son
[Borlum Branch & fam. of Raigmore]
Duncan 5th Son
[Aberarder Branch]
Lachlan 7th Son
[Corribrough Branch]
18 17 Sir Lachlan d. 1620
= Annas Grant of Freuchie
19 18 William = Margaret Graham
d. 1660 of Fintry
Lachlan of Kinrara
no male issue
Angus of Daviot
= Marjory Robertson of Inshes
20 19 Lachlan d. 1704
= Margaret Lindsay of Edzell
Lachlan of Daviot
= Anna Mackenzie of Redcastle
Alexander
= Anne Fraser of Culduthel
21 20 Lachlan d. s.p. 1731
= Anne Duff of Drummuir
22 21 William
d. s.p. 1740
23 22 Æneas or Angus d. s.p. 1770
= Ann Farquharson of Invercauld
Alexander
= —Davidson
Duncan of Castle Leathers
= Agnes Dallas of Cantray
24 23 Sir Æneas = Margaret Grant
d. s.p. 1820 of Dalvey
25 24 Alexander
d unm. 1827
26 25 Angus d. 1833
= Archange St. Martin

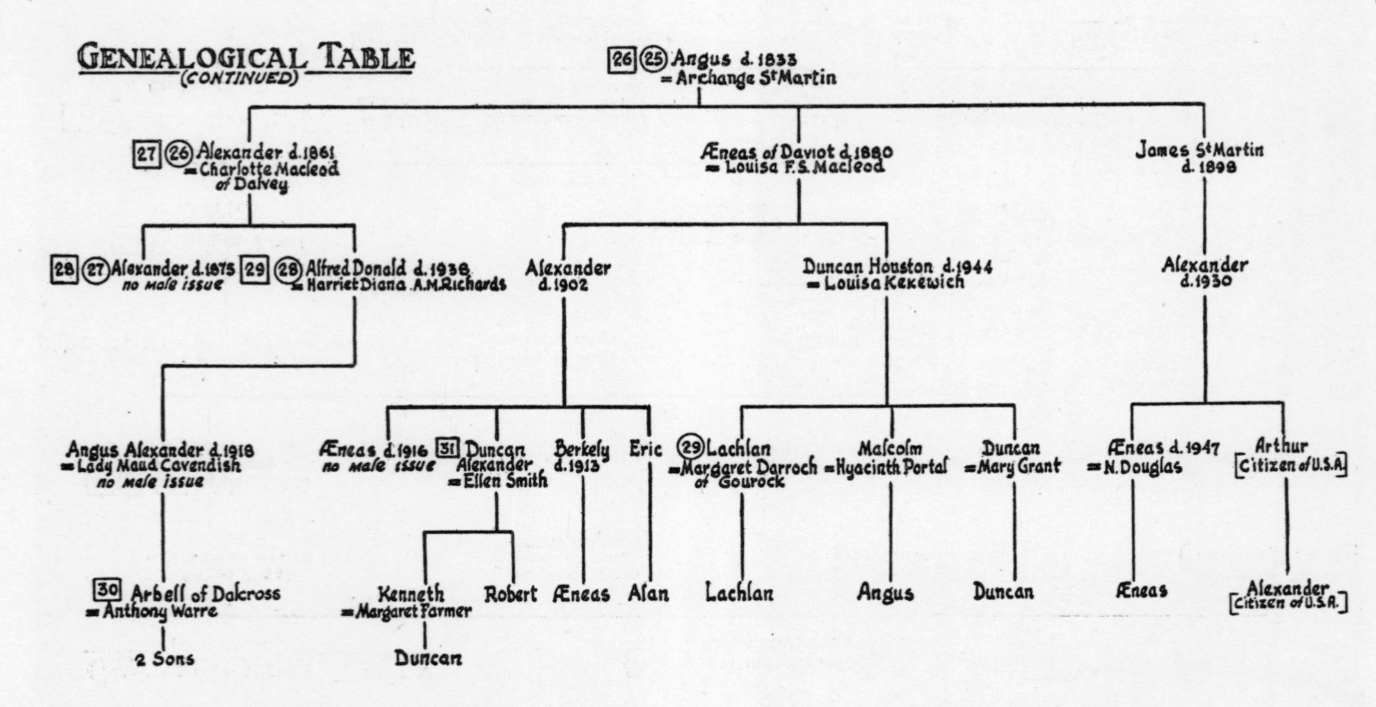
GENEALOGICAL TABLE
(CONTINUED)
26 25 Angus d. 1833
= Archange St Martin
27 26 Alexander d. 1861
= Charlotte Macleod of Dalvey
Æneas of Daviot d. 1880
= Louisa F.S. Macleod
James St Martin d. 1898
28 27 Alexander d. 1875 no male issue
29 28 Alfred Donald d. 1938
= Harriet Diana A.M. Richards
Alexander d. 1902
Duncan Houston d. 1944
= Louisa Kekewich
Alexander d. 1930
Angus Alexander d. 1918
= Lady Maud Cavendish
no male issue
Æneas d. 1916 no male issue
31 Duncan Alexander
= Ellen Smith
Berkely d. 1913
Eric
29 Lachlan
= Margaret Darroch of Gourock
Malcolm
= Hyacinth Portal
Duncan
= Mary Grant
Æneas d. 1947
= N. Douglas
Arthur
[Citizen of U.S.A.]
30 Arbell of Dalcross
= Anthony Warre
Kenneth
= Margaret Farmer
Robert
Æneas
Alan
Lachlan
Angus
Duncan
Æneas
Alexander
[Citizen of U.S.A.]
2 Sons
Duncan

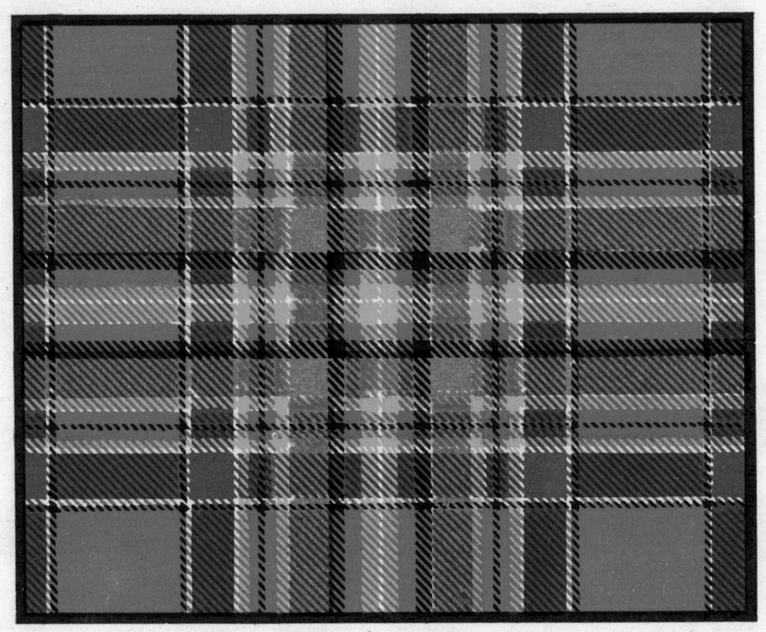

CLAN CHATTAN

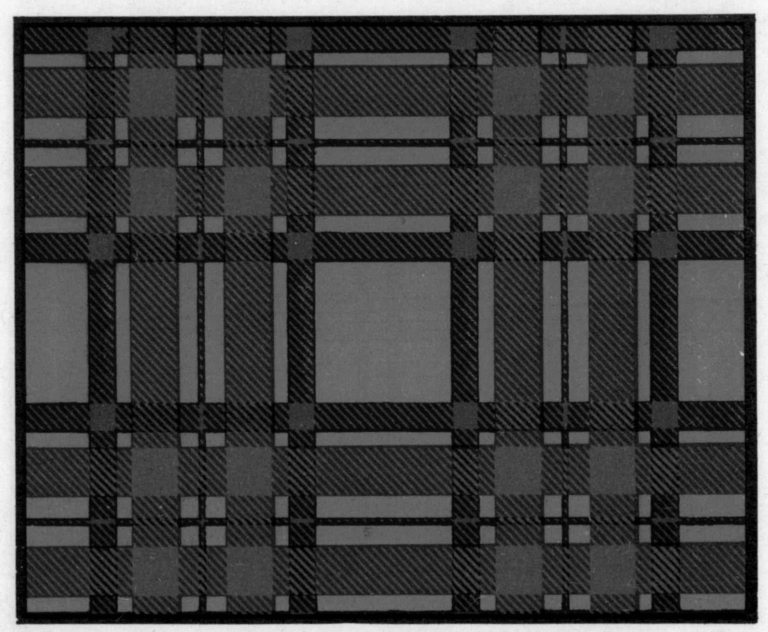

MACKINTOSH

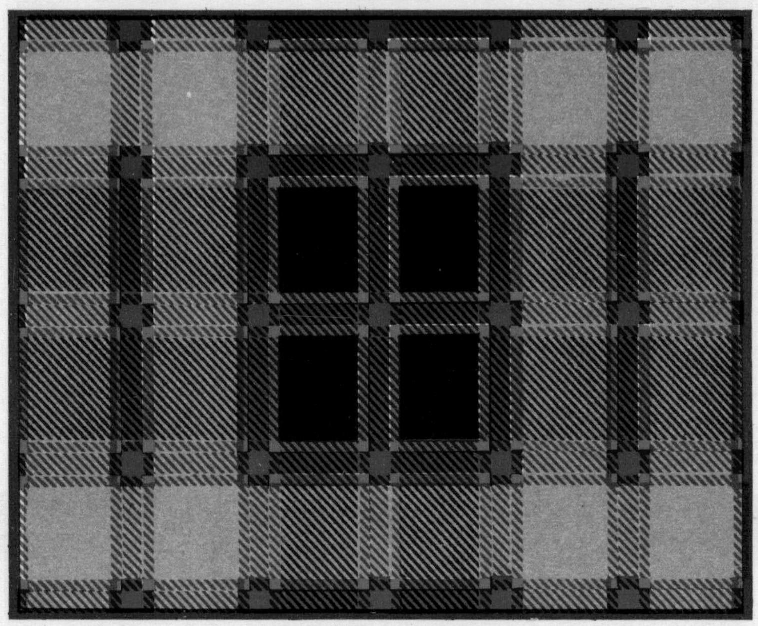

MACPHERSON, Hunting

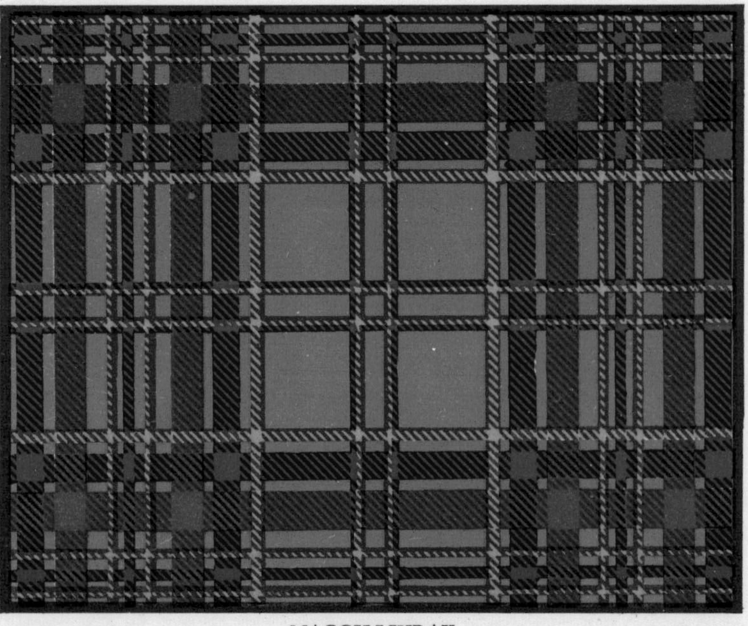

MACGILLIVRAY

APPENDIX I

PRINCIPAL BRANCHES OF CLAN MACKINTOSH

Kyllachy, with off-shoots of Holm, Dalmigavie, Farr
Borlum, with off-shoots of Raigmore
Aberarder
Corribrough
Strone and Gask, with off-shoots of Balnespick and Balvraid
Connage (Clan Eachin)

OTHER TRIBES AND FAMILIES OF CLAN MACKINTOSH

Shaw, with off-shoots of Rothiemurchus, Dell, Kinrara, Guislich, Tordarroch, Dalnavert, Inchrory
Shaws or M'Ays of Black Isle
Shaws of Aberdeen, Perthshire and the Isles
Farquharsons
Clan Fearchair or Fhionnlaidh or Fionlay
of Whitehouse
,, Allargue
,, Haughton
,, Finzean
Farquharsons—contd.
of Breda
,, Tullycairn
,, Allanquoich
,, Inverie.
,, Invercauld
,, Brouchdearg
,, Monaltrie
,, Achriachan
Mackintosh of Dalmunzie (Clan Ritchie)
M'Combies or Clan Thomas (Mackintoshes of Glenshie)

CLANS OF THE BLOOD OF CLAN CHATTAN

Macphersons or Clan Mhuirich
of Cluny
,, Nuid
,, Blairgowrie
,, Balavil
,, Brin
,, Breakachie
,, Ballachoran
,, Pitmean, with off-shoots of Strathmashie, Garramore, Invertrumie, Biallid, Pitchern
,, Invereshie
Macphersons—contd.
of Phoiness
,, Dellifour
,, Killihuntly
Cattanachs
Macbeans or Clan Vean
of Faillie
,, Tomatin
,, Drummond
,, Wester Drakies
,, Dores
Macphails or Clan Phail
of Invernairnie

OTHER CLANS WHO HAVE JOINED CLAN CHATTAN

Macgillivrays
Davidsons or Clan Dhaibhidh
or *Dhai*
of Tulloch
„ Cantray
„ Inchmarlow
Macleans of Dochgarroch
or Clan Tearlich
Macleans of the North
Clan Tarril
Smiths or Gows
Macqueens or Clan Revan
of Pollochaig
„ Clune
„ Strathnoon
Clan Andrish
Clarks or Clan Chlerich
Macintyres of Badenoch
Macandrews

SEPTS OF CLAN CHATTAN

Clan Mackintosh

Adamson
Ayson
Clark
Clarke
Clarkson
Clerk
Combie
Crerar
Dallas
Doles
Elder
Esson
Glen
Glennie
Hardie
Hardy
MacAndrew
MacAy
MacCardney
MacChlerich
MacChlery
MacComb
MacCombie
MaComie
MacOmie
M'Conchy
MacFall
Macglashan
Machardie
Machardy
MacHay
MacKeggie
M'Killican
MacLerie
MacNiven
MacPhail
Macritchie
MacThomas
Macvail
Niven
Noble
Paul
Ritchie
Shaw
Tarrill
Tosh
Toshach

Clan Macpherson

Cattanach
Clark
Clarke
Clarkson
Clerk
Currie
Fersen
Gillespie
Gillies
Gow
Keith
Lees
MacChlerich
MacChlery
MacCurrach
MacGowan
MacKeith
MacLeish
Maclerie
MacLise
MacMurdo
MacMurdoch
MacMurrich
MacVurrich
Murdoch
Murdoson

Clan Macbean

Bean
MacBeath
MacBeth
Macilvain
MacVean

Clan Farquharson

Coutts
Farquhar
Findlay
Findlayson
Finlay
Finlayson
Grevsach
Hardie
Hardy
Leys
Lyon
MacCaig
MacCardney
MacEaracher
MacFarquhar
MacGuaig
Machardie
MacKerchar
MacKerracher
Mackinlay
Reoch
Riach

Clan Davidson

Davie	Dawson	MacDade	MacDavid
Davis	Dow	Macdaid	Kay

Clan Macgillivray

Gilroy	MacGilroy	MacGilvray	Macilvrae
MacGillivoor	MacGilvra	Macilroy	

Clan Macqueen

MacCunn	MacSween	MacSwyde	Swan
MacSwan	MacSwen		

Clan Shaw

Macleans of Dochgarroch

Macintyres of Badenoch

APPENDIX II

MISCELLANEOUS NOTES

TITLE OF THE CHIEF

Chiefs of clans doubled their patronymic to emphasize their chiefship. The older title of the Chief of Mackintosh is " Mackintosh of that Ilk " or " Mackintosh of Mackintosh." The Chief is now known as " The Mackintosh of Mackintosh " or, in brief, " The Mackintosh."

When the Chief of Mackintosh became Chief of Clan Chattan in 1291 he was also known as " Mackintosh of Torcastle." From about 1500 to 1600 the Chief of Mackintosh was called " Mackintosh of Dunachton."

The present Chief or Captain of Clan Chattan is known as " Mackintosh of Mackintosh-Torcastle."

THE SPELLING OF THE NAME OF MACKINTOSH

There has been some controversy how this name should be spelt. The name has been spelt in fifty different ways in the course of the last five hundred years, but the Chief has spelt it MACKINTOSH for the last couple of hundred years. The following are some of the various forms of spelling :

Mac-an-toisich	Makinthoschey	Mc yntosach	M'Kintoschis
Macintoshich	Makyntoische	Mc yntose	M'Kintoschissone
Mac Toshy	Makyntoshe	Mc ynchosse	M'Kintoisch
Macintosh	Makin Toshie	M'Colmetoshe	M'Kyntoshe
Mackintoche	Malcomtosh	M'Intosche	M'Kyntoschey
Mackintoshie	Malcometoshe	M'intosh	M'Kyntoysschis
MacIntosh	Makynthoschey	M'Intosh	M'Kyntoshy
Mackintosh	Mc anetosche	M'Intoshe	M'Kyntosy
Makintoshe	Mc Kintoche	M'Intoschie	M'yntossich
Makintoich	Mc Intosche	M'inthosych	M'yntosche
Makkintoshe	Mc Intoshe	M'Kintoshe	M'Kynthoschey
Makintoishe	Mc intosh	M'Kintosshe	
Makintosche	Mc Intosh	M'Kintosche	

Mackintosh Clan War Cry is " Loch Moigh " (Moy) [Loch of the Plain].

Pipe Music. The following pipe tunes belong to the Clans :

Clan Chattan . The Gathering—" The Black Rock of Clan Chattan."
Mackintosh . The Gathering—" The Mackintosh's Banner."
Mackintosh . Lament—" The Mackintosh's Lament."

It is not certain if the Lament was written on the death of William, 13th Chief, who was murdered in 1550 by Lady Huntly at Bog-o'-Giht, or of Sir Lachlan, 17th Chief, who died suddenly at Gartenbeg in 1622.

Clan Tartans. There is a Mackintosh tartan, a chief of Clan Chattan tartan and a Clan Chattan tartan. The tartan of the chief of Clan Chattan is identical with the Clan Chattan tartan except that it is crossed by additional white lines which meet in the centres of the main red squares, and thus divide each of these squares into four equal parts.

There is no authorized Mackintosh hunting tartan.

Clan Badge of Mackintosh and Clan Chattan is the Red Whortleberry. Boxwood has been used as a substitute in the absence of the proper plant.

Wadset. An old Scots variant of the mortgage in which the person lending the money was allowed to occupy the land until he received payment.

Heraldry. The original arms of the Mackintosh Chiefs in 1490 were a "Lion Rampant" (to denote their descent from MacDuff, Earl of Fife), and with this is quartered a "Lymphad," or galley, indicating the Mackintoshes' descent from and inheritance of the Clan Chattan.

By 1530 there appears in the shield "a hand fessways holding a heart paleways in Chief," which is The Mackintosh's own armorial bearing, and a wolf's head, or perhaps a boar's, erased in base, is noted on a seal. This is possibly the first appearance of a boar's head couped, which in 1543 becomes a quartering in the shield of William, 13th Chief, as heir-of-line of the Gordons of Lochinvar.

In 1672, as Chief of the Clan Chattan, The Mackintosh received a matriculation of the Clan Chattan galley with the hand and heart in Chief, but evidently this was not considered properly indicative of the two chiefships, viz., of Mackintosh and of Clan Chattan.

Accordingly, in 1679, the arms of the Chief of Mackintosh were remarshalled in a matriculation by the Lord Lyon, as follows:

Quarterly—1. *or* a lion rampant *gu*;
2. *arg* a dexter hand couped fessways grasping a man's heart paleways *gu*;
3. *azure* a boar's head couped *or*;
4. *or* a lymphad, her oars in saltire (properly azure).

Crest—A cat salient *proper*; with Supporters two cats proper, and Motto "Touch not the Catt but (without) a glove."

By Statutory Confirmation of 25th April 1947, the Lord Lyon confirmed to Duncan A. E. Mackintosh of Mackintosh-Torcastle and Clan Chattan as (31st) Chief of the Clan Chattan, the following arms:

Quarterly, 1st, Or, a lion rampant Gules (for Macduff); 2nd, Argent, a dexter hand couped fessways, holding a heart in pale Gules, a label Azure in chief charged with three bulls' heads cabossed of the first for difference (for Mackintosh); 3rd, Azure a boar's head couped Or, armed proper, langued Gules; 4th, Or, a lymphad, sails furled, oars in saltire Azure, flagged Gules (for Clan Chattan), over all an inescutcheon *en surtout* charged as the fourth for Captain or Chief of the Clan Chattan; above the shield is placed an Helmet befitting his degree with a Mantling Azure doubled Or, and on a Wreath of these Liveries is set for Crest a cat salient proper (for Clan Chattan) and in an Escrol over the same this Motto TOUCH NOT THE CATT BUT A GLOVE, and on a compartment below the Shield embellished with red whortleberry, being a badge-plant of the Clan Chattan, along with this Slughorn (war cry), CLANN CHATTAN, are set for Supporters two grey cats salient proper.

The label in the second quarter indicates that he is not Chief of Clan Mackintosh, whilst the small shield *en surtout* with the blue galley, denotes him to be Chief of the " haill kin of Clan Chattan."

By similar certificate, of date 9th June 1947, the Lord Lyon confirmed to Rear-Admiral Lachlan Donald Mackintosh of Mackintosh the following arms, denoting him to be The Mackintosh of Mackintosh and Chief of Clan Mackintosh, viz. :

Quarterly, 1st, Or, a lion rampant Gules, armed and langued Azure ; 2nd, Argent, a dexter hand couped fessways grasping a man's heart paleways Gules ; 3rd, Azure a boar's head couped Or, armed proper and langued Gules ; 4th, Or, a lymphad, sails furled Azure, flagged and surmounted of her oars in saltire Gules ; above the Shield is placed an Helmet befitting his degree with a Mantling Gules doubled Or, and on a Wreath of these Liveries is set for Crest a cat-a-mountain salient guardant proper, and in an Escrol over the same this Motto LOCH MOIGH, and on a compartment below the shield embellished with red whortleberry fructed proper, as being the badge of the Clan Mackintosh, along with this Motto TOUCH NOT THE CAT BOT A GLOVE, are set for Supporters two cat-a-mountains guardant proper.

The banners of the respective Chiefs, indicating their presence or authority, are the rectangular flags of which the whole surface is emblazoned with the same device as appear on their shields (that of the Chief of Clan Chattan displaying his inescutcheon in its centre). Their standards or standing flags (*vide* coloured illustration of Clan Chattan standard) are hoisted at Gatherings beside the Chief's pavilion during the day, their banners being only raised when they become personally present or represented by their commissioner.

CLAN CHATTAN ASSOCIATION

This association has for its object to promote friendly social intercourse amongst members of the clans and septs of Clan Chattan. All persons of either sex bearing the name of and/or being descended from any of the clans or septs of the Clan Chattan, or having historical territorial connection with the Clan Chattan country, shall be eligible as members. The Secretary is Herbert Mackintosh, Esq., Annandale, Lower Bourne, Farnham, Surrey.

APPENDIX III

LIST OF RELICS AT MOY

1. Sword dated 1504 of Viscount Dundee, worn by him at Killiecrankie 1689, and given by the Graham family to the 19th Chief.
2. Sword given by Prince Charles (afterwards Charles I) to Sir Lachlan, the 17th Chief.
3. Sword of Pope Leo X, given by James V to the 15th Chief in 1538.
4. Sword belonging to Donald Fraser, blacksmith, at Moy, and Captain of the Five at the Rout of Moy, 1746.
5. Anvil belonging to Donald Fraser.
6. Highland Claymore, with Basket Hilt, from the battlefield of Culloden.
7. Cavalry sword found on Culloden Moor.
8. Bonnet of Prince Charles—left at Moy Hall on morning of Monday, 17th February 1746, about 5 a.m., when Lord Loudon intended to surprise the Prince.
9. Bed in which Prince Charles slept during his stay at Moy Hall, February 1746.
10. Domino box of William, Duke of Cumberland in 1746, made of walrus ivory and bone. The Royal insignia and monogram are cut from solid ivory.
11. Gold watch belonging to Mary Queen of Scots.
12. Jacobite toast glass (eighteenth century), on which is cut the Rose, emblematic of the British monarchy, and the Butterfly, of new young life.
13. China cup out of which Prince Charles took tea.
14. Collection of seven Rose Jacobite medals.
15. Piece of tartan from Prince Charles's plaid.
16. Prince Charles's button.
17. Framed letter of Prince Charles.
18. Rod " Main de Justice " of Charles Rex.
19. Knife and fork found in Queen Mary's house, Inverness.
20. Oak casket containing Freedom of Royal Burgh of Inverness, 1925, with gold ring of Free Burgess, given to 28th Chief.
21. Bamboo cane walking-stick with silver mount, given by King George V to 28th Chief.
22. Silver ink stand with Royal crest, presented in 1911 by King George V to 28th Chief.
23. Silver cigarette case presented to 28th Chief by the Prince of Wales (later King George V).
24. Set of crystal and gold-backed cuff links with Prince of Wales feathers and Royal monogram, presented to 28th Chief by the Prince of Wales (later King George V).
25. Diamond scarf pin with Prince of Wales crest, given to 28th Chief by the Prince of Wales (later King George V).

26. Portrait of William, 18th Chief.
27. Portrait of Lachlan, 20th Chief.
28. Portrait of Sir Æneas, 23rd Chief.
29. Portrait of Angus, 25th Chief.
30. Portrait of Alfred Donald, 28th Chief.
31. Portrait of Ann Duff, wife of 20th Chief.
32. Portrait of Lady Mackintosh, wife of 23rd Chief.
33. Seal with coat of arms.
34. Snuffmull of James V, given by him to the 15th Chief.
35. Chief of Mackintosh's banner, with coat of arms.
36. Book of tartans collected in 1848.
37. Collection of pistols, claymores, etc., and relics from the battlefield of Culloden and Mulroy.
38. Manuscript of Sir Æneas, 23rd Chief; manuscript of Rev. Lachlan Shaw, 1758; manuscript of Lachlan of Kinrara, 1679; and other histories of the Mackintoshes.
39. Two swords used in the battle of the North Inch of Perth, 1396.
40. Piece of scarf worn by Prince Charles at Edinburgh Castle, 1745.
41. Emblazonment of Arms of the 29th Chief, carved in wood by John McLay in 1947.

MAPS

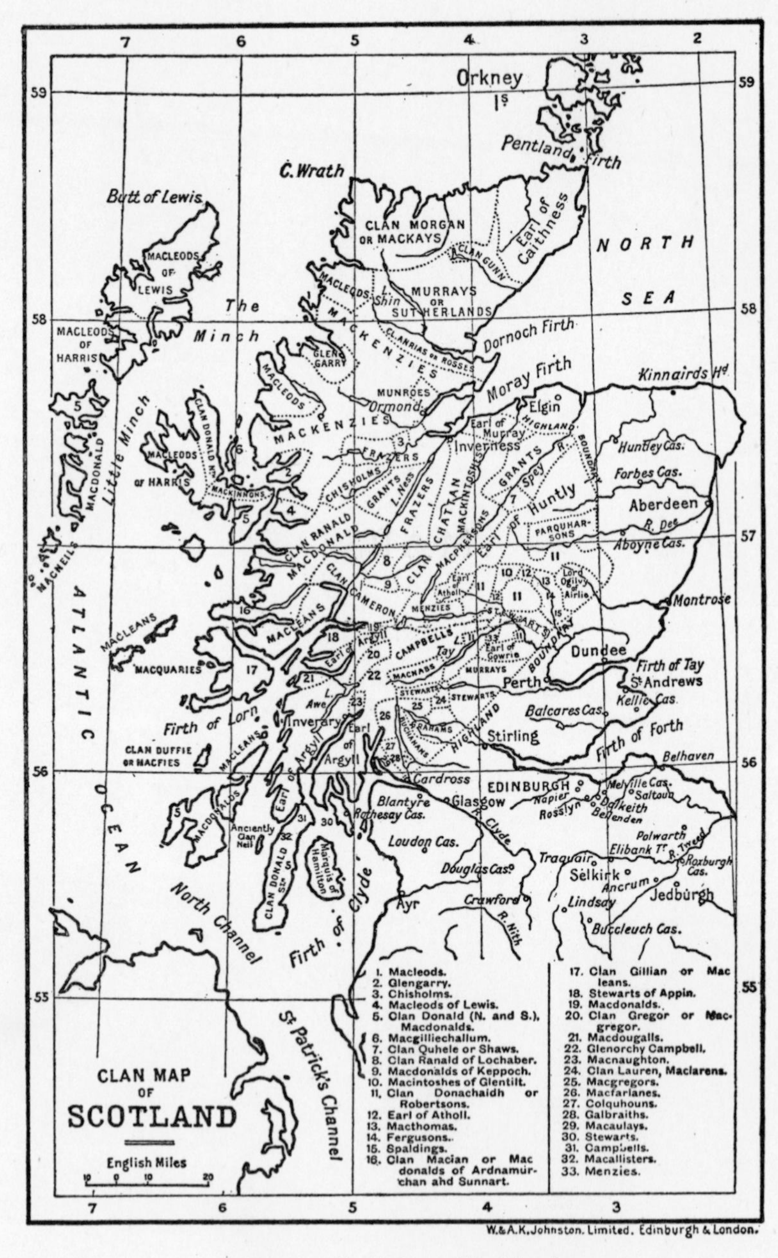

Map 1. Clan Map of Scotland.

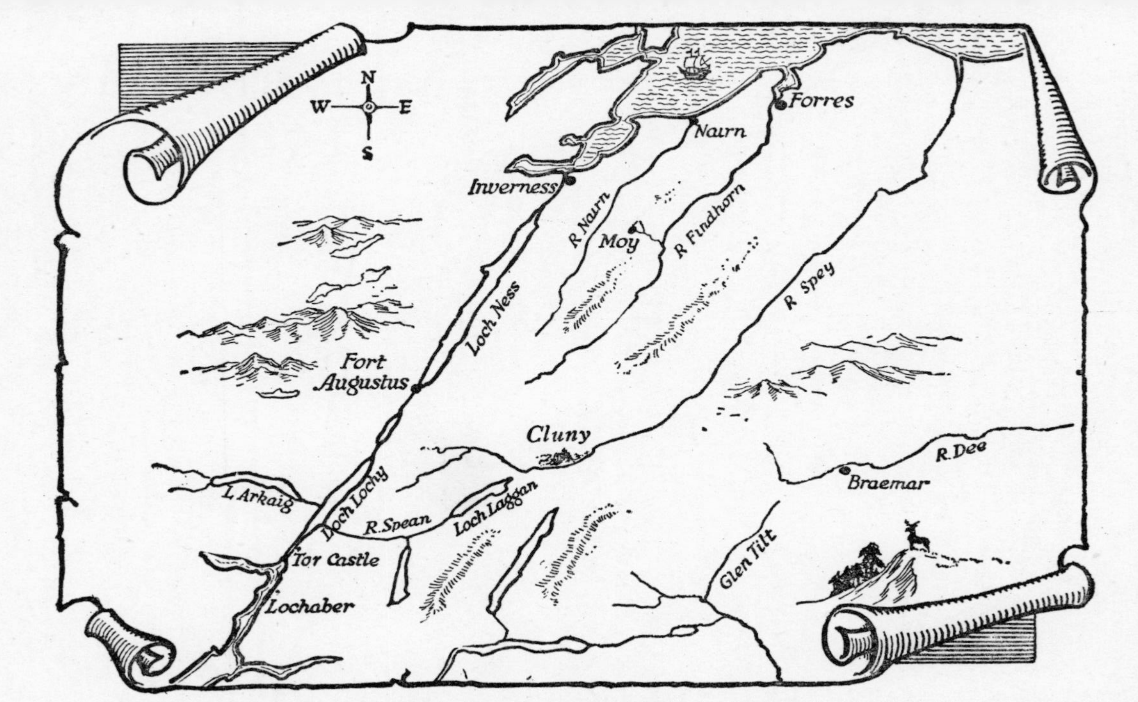

Map 2. Clan Chattan Country. The Nairn Valley, in which the Battlefield of Culloden is situate, was of old the chief habitat of MacGillivrays, MacBeans, MacPhails, Davidsons and many smaller septs. The Findhorn Valley was, and still is, the Mackintosh stronghold, where MacQueens and others intimately connected with the land are still to be found. Mackintosh influence reaches to the shores of Loch Lochy. The Spey is the home of Shaws, Clarks, Cattanachs and Mackintoshes in its lower portion, and the Macphersons hold the upper reaches. Farquharsons were across the Cairngorms on the waters of the Dee. Ritchies lived south of the Grampians on a tributary of the Tay.

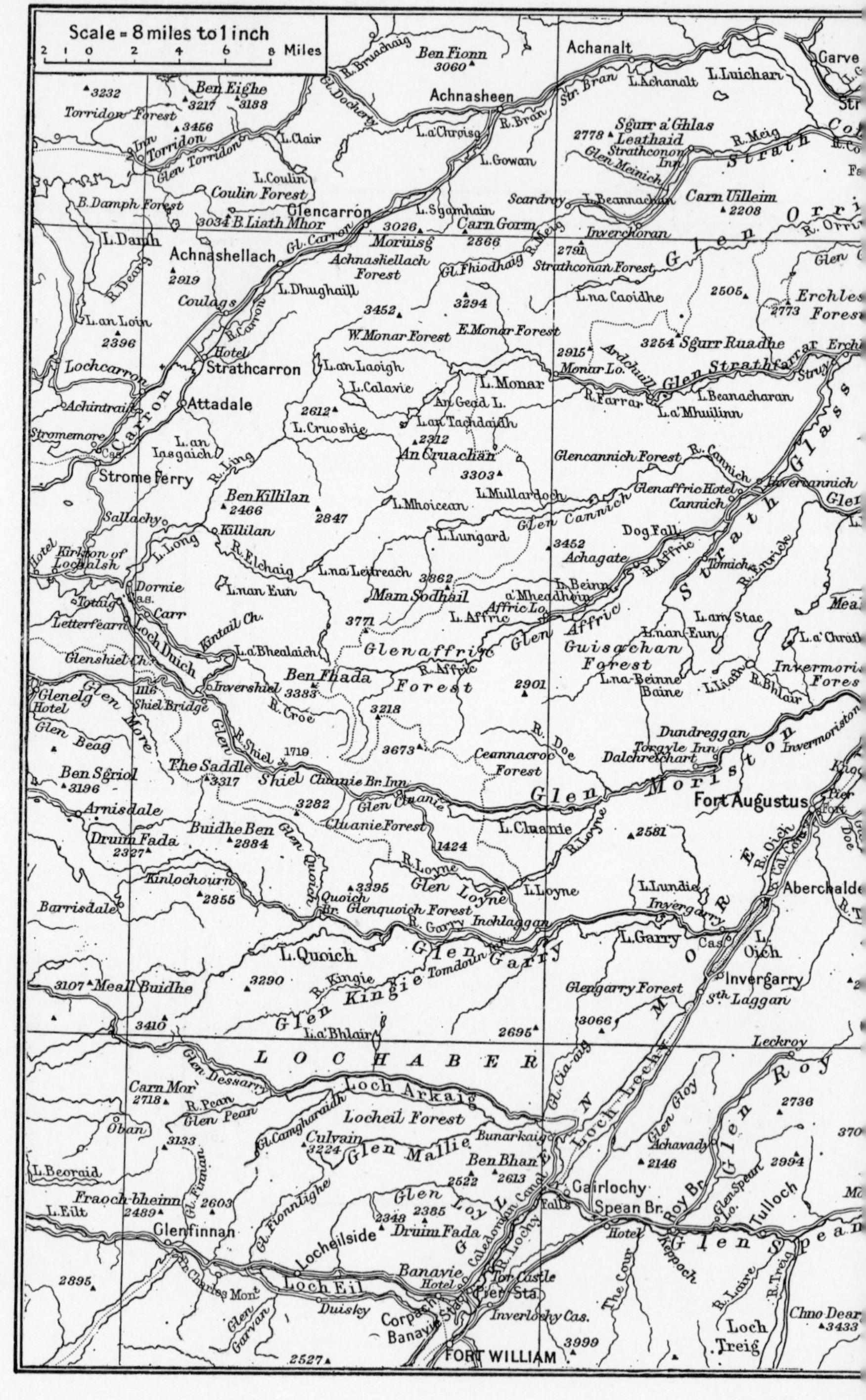

Map 3. Clan Chattan Coun

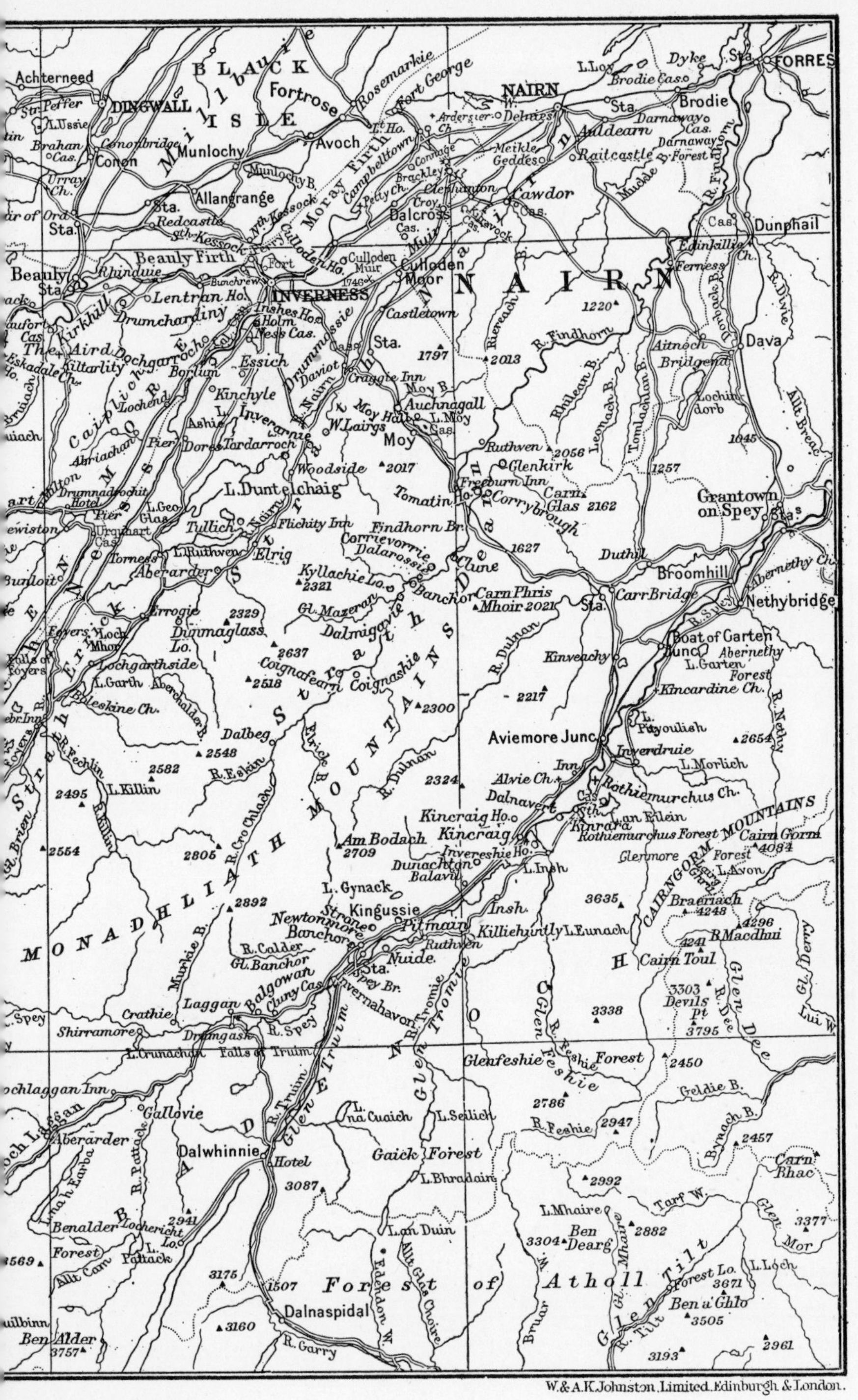

W. & A. K. Johnston, Limited, Edinburgh & London.

nd Neighourhood.

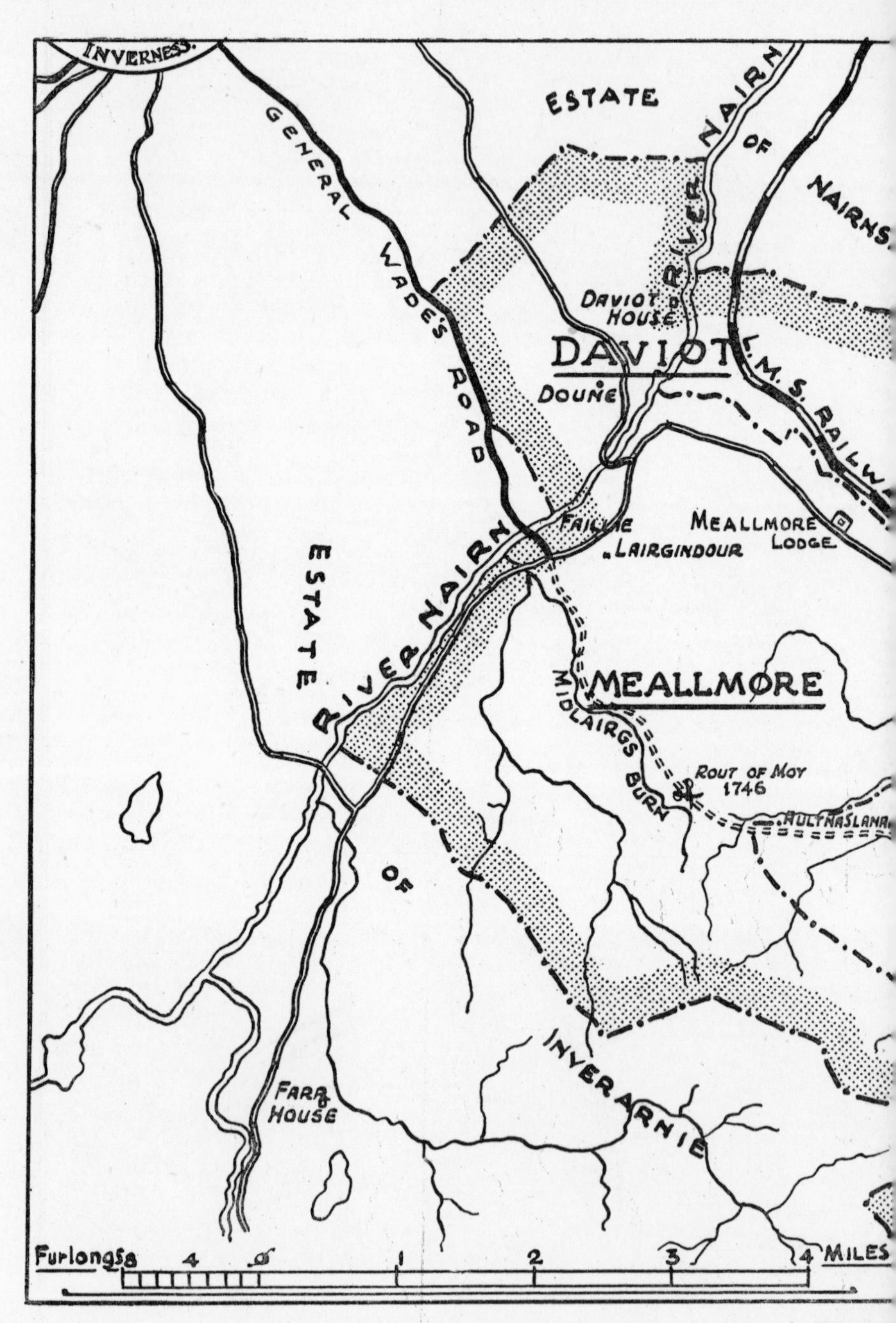

Map 4. Estates of Daviot

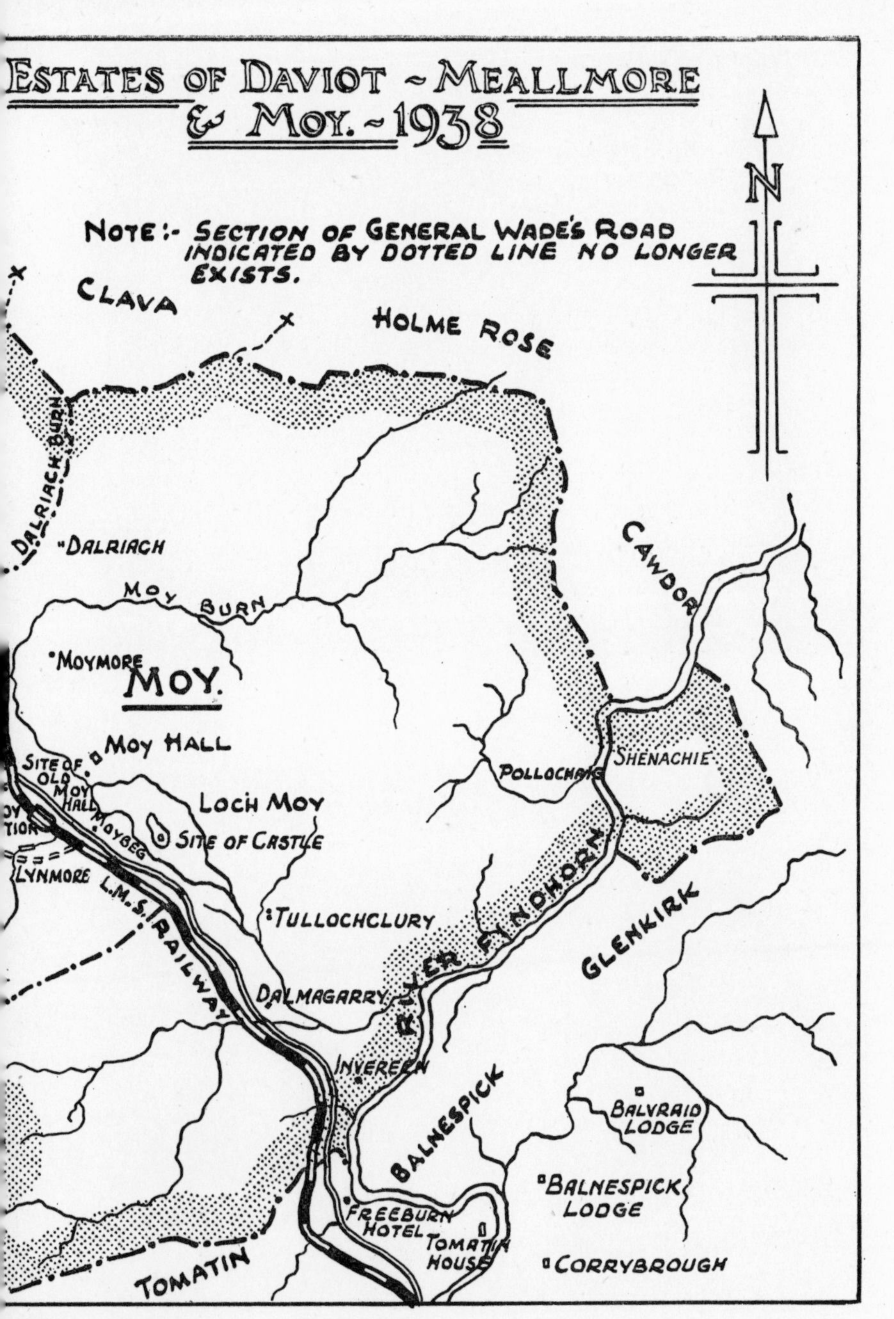

Meallmore and Moy.

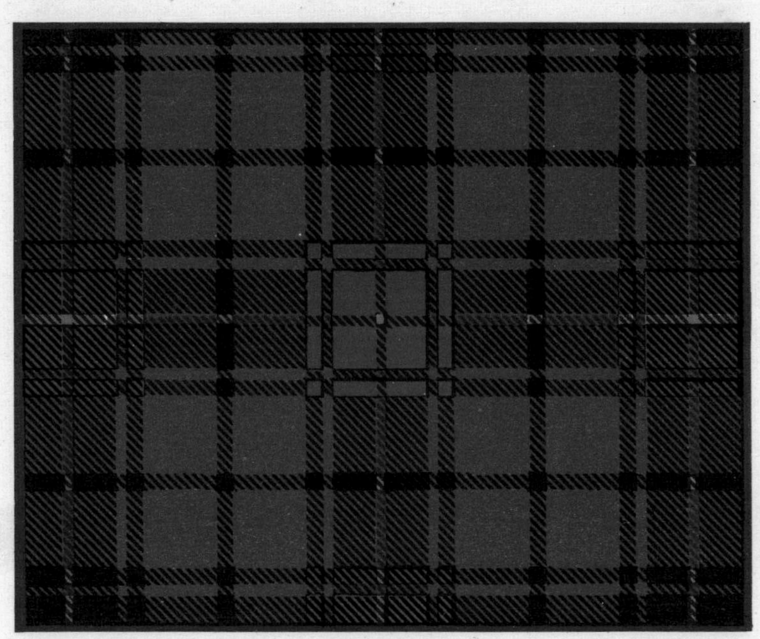

DAVIDSON

MACQUEEN

MACBEAN

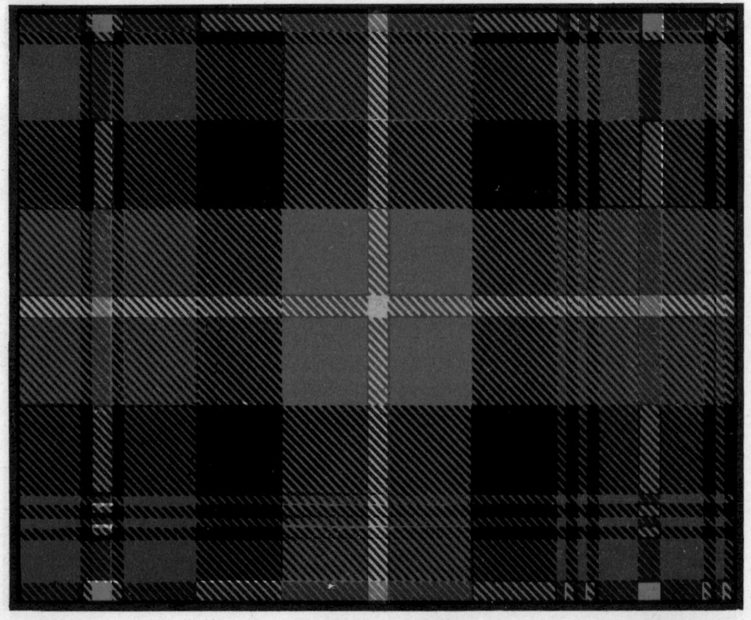

FARQUHARSON

1. Battle of the North Inch at Perth, 1396, was fought by thirty of the Clan Chattan against thirty Camerons to settle their feud. (Picture of a tapestry.) There were four Tapestries in the drawing-room at Moy, made in Halkin Street, London, to the order of Arabella, wife of the 28th Chief, in 1890.

2. Massacre of the Comyns, about 1424. The Mackintoshes were invited to a feast by the Comyns, but were warned beforehand of treachery, for which the signal was to be the entry of a black bull's head. When the bull's head was brought in the Mackintoshes forestalled the Comyns and slew them all. (Picture of a tapestry.)

3. William, 15th Chief, had been tried for conspiracy by Lord Huntly and was condemned to death. The sentence was carried out by Lady Huntly in her husband's absence, and she had William beheaded at Bog o' Giht in 1550. (Picture of a tapestry.)

4. Lady Mackintosh, wife of 22nd Chief, raised a regiment of Mackintoshes for Prince Charles in 1745, and entertained him at Moy Hall in 1746. (Picture of a tapestry. By courtesy of Major James Caldwell, J.P., of Carrbridge, Inverness-shire.)

5. William, 18th Chief, 1622–1660. "A man distinguished for piety, just and equitable in his conduct, faithful to his word and of dignified behaviour and good manners."

6. Lachlan, 20th Chief, 1704–1731, "of a middle stature, ruddy complexion, straight and lively. He was a most firm friend, kind master and indulgent chief." He took part in the Jacobite rising of 1715, and was imprisoned in London.

7. Ann Duff, wife of Lachlan, 20th Chief. She entertained Prince Charles at her house in Inverness in 1746. Later, the Duke of Cumberland took her house as his headquarters. Lady Mackintosh used to say, " I have had two King's bairns living with me in my time, and to tell you the truth I wish I may never have another."

8. Brigadier William Mackintosh of Borlum, hero of 1715
An outstanding character.

9. Lady Mackintosh, née Anne Farquharson of Invercauld, wife of Angus, 22nd Chief. She was a heroine of the Jacobite Rising in 1745.

10. Sir Æneas, 23rd Chief, 1770–1820. He was created a baronet by King George III, because of his good influence and high position in the Highlands.

11. Angus, 25th Chief, 1827–1833, great-grandfather of Duncan Alexander, 31st Chief of Clan Chattan, and Lachlan, 29th Chief of Mackintosh.

12. Alexander, 26th Chief, 1833–1861. " A Mackintosh to the backbone."

13. Alexander Æneas, 27th Chief, 1861–1875. A popular Chief.
He greatly enlarged Moy Hall.

14. Alfred Donald, 28th Chief, 1875–1938. A great Chief of honoured memory.

15. H.M. King George V with The Mackintosh and Mr. Lloyd George at Moy Hall, September 1921.

16. Rear-Admiral Lachlan Donald Mackintosh of Mackintosh, C.B., D.S.O., D.S.C., 29th Chief. *(Photo by Drummond Young.)*

17. Margaret, wife of 29th Chief, author of this book
(*Photo by Harrods Ltd.*)

18. Lachlan Ronald Duncan Mackintosh of Mackintosh Younger.
(Photo by Vandyk.)

19. Prince Charles Edward Stuart, by John Pettie, reproduced by gracious permission of His Majesty the King. Cameron of Lochiel is on the left of the picture and on the right is the figure usually called Forbes of Pitsligo, but which may possibly be Macdonald of Clan Ranald.

20. Bed slept in by Prince Charles at Moy Hall, 16th February 1746.
(*Photo by D. Whyte.*)

21. Anvil and Sword of Donald Fraser, hero of the Rout of Moy, 1746.
(Photo by D. Whyte.)

22. Battle of Culloden, 1746, by David Morier, reproduced by gracious permission of His Majesty the King. This picture was painted for the Duke of Cumberland, and shows Barrell's regiment being attacked by Highlanders, some of whom are wearing Mackintosh tartan.

23. Battlefield of Culloden, with memorial cairn and some of the gravestones marking the massed graves.

24. One of three gravestones in memory of the Mackintosh clansmen on Culloden Moor.

25. Mackintosh in Highland Court Dress of eighteenth century.
(From *M'Ian's Highlanders.* Published 1847.)

26. Alexander Mackintosh, born 1842, Ground Officer. Archibald Mackintosh, born 1827, Farm Manager. They both held their offices on the Mackintosh Estates. (From *Highlanders of Scotland*, by Kenneth Macleay. Published 1870.)

27. Cluny Macpherson in full dress.
(From *M'Ian's Highlanders.*)

28. Fearchar Farquharson, aged 115, with his Lochaber axe.
(From *M'Ian's Highlanders.*)

29. Macgillivray with belted plaid.
(From *M'Ian's Highlanders.*)

30. Gillies Macbean defending the breach in the wall at Culloden.
(From *M'Ian's Highlanders*. Published 1847.)

31. Davidson.
(From *M'Ian's Highlanders.*)

32. Old Moy Hall, sketched by Sir Æneas Mackintosh about 1775. It was built about 1700 and burned down about 1800.

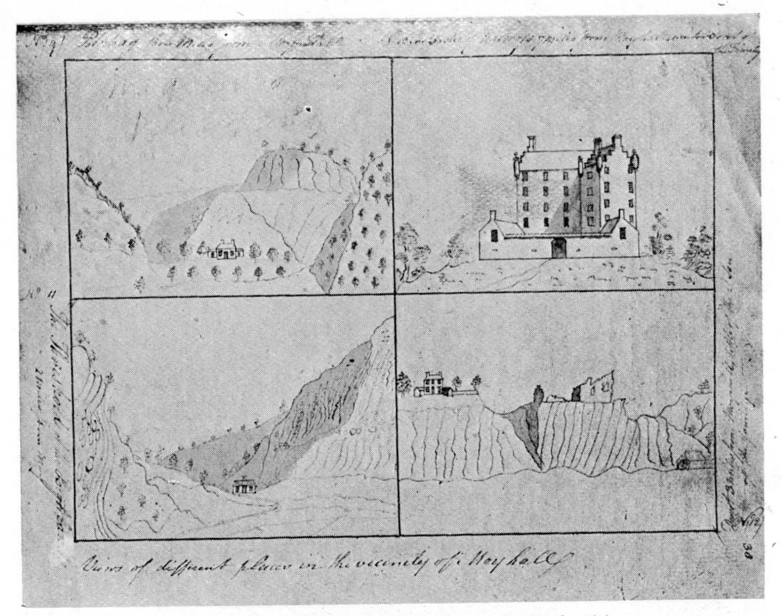

33. Sketches by Sir Æneas Mackintosh, 23rd Chief, with notes.

Top left—Polochag, 3 miles from Moy Hall.

Top right—The Castle of Dalcross, 7 miles from Moy Hall, winter seat of the family.

Bottom left—The Threshold of the Highlands, 2 miles from Moy.

Bottom right—Daviot, 3 miles from Moy Hall, the seat of the second son of the family.

34. Loch Moy from the South, showing Ben Wyvis in the background.

35. Loch Moy from the North, with view of Cairngorms.

36. Moy Hall from the South. The walled garden is to the left and the site of the old house was between the garden and the Loch.

37. Moy Hall, overlooking Loch Moy, with a beautiful view towards the Cairngorm Mountains. The centre is the original house, which was built about 1800. The Tower and block on left were added by the 27th Chief. (*Photo by Drummond Young.*)

38. Moy Hall—west view.
(Photo by Drummond Young.)

39. Dining-room in Moy Hall.

40. Island in Loch Moy, with monument to Sir Æneas, 23rd Chief.
The site of the old Castle is to the right.

41. Loch an Eilean with the Castle, an ancient stronghold and home of Shaw, 4th Chief, and later of the Shaws of Rothiemurchus.
From a picture in the Smoking-room at Moy Hall.

42. Daviot House, built about 1820, by Alexander, 24th Chief.

43. Meallmore Lodge, built in 1869 by Alexander, 27th Chief.

44. Glenspean Lodge, built by Alfred, 28th Chief, in 1923.

45. Coignafearn Lodge on River Findhorn. The Lodge was built about 1900, and is 1500 ft. above sea-level.

1. Sword (dated 1504) of Viscount Dundee, used at Killiecrankie, 1689, where Dundee was killed. This sword was afterwards given to the 19th Chief.

2. Sword of King Charles I, given by him when Prince of Wales, to the 17th Chief in 1622.

3. Ancient Claymore used at the Battle of the North Inch at Perth, 1396.

4. Sword of Pope Leo X, given by James V to the 15th Chief in 1538.

5. Snuff mull of James V, King of Scots, given by him to the 15th Chief.

6. Watch of Mary, Queen of Scots.

7. Bonnet of Prince Charles which he left at Moy, 1746.

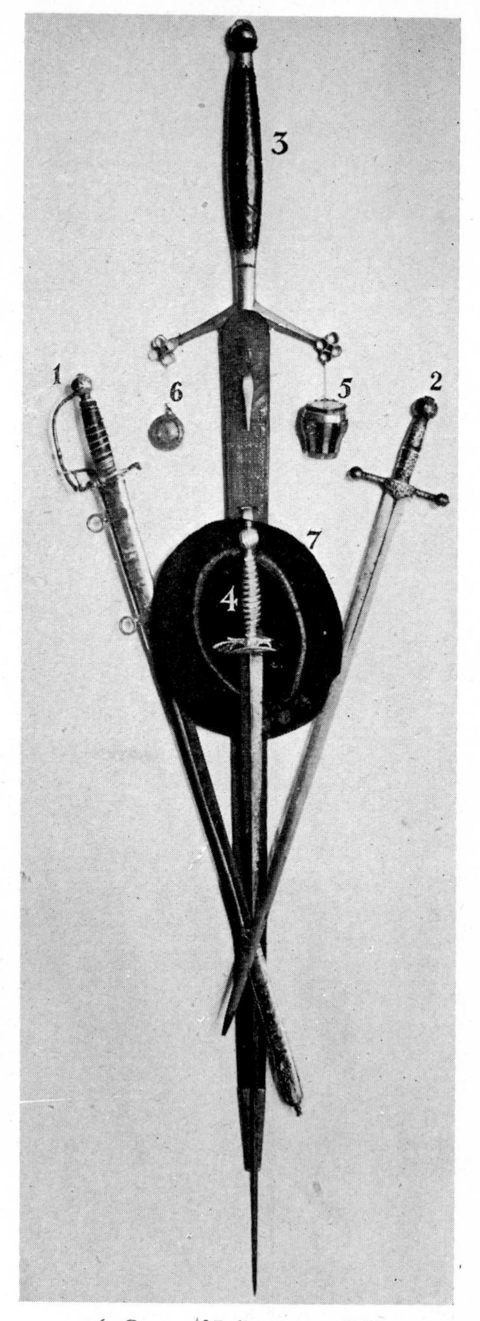

46. Group of Relics at Moy Hall.

47. Chief of Mackintosh's banner, with coat of arms.

48. Official Emblazonment of the Arms of "Lauchlane McKintosh of that Ilk alias of Torcastle," 19th Chief of Mackintosh and 20th Chief of Clan Chattan as matriculated in Lyon Register, March, 1679.